HACKS FOR

TIKTOK

150 TIPS AND TRICKS

for Editing and Posting Videos, Getting Likes, Keeping Your Fans Happy, and Making Money

KYLE BRACH

Racehorse Publishing

Racehorse Publishing books may be purchased in bulk at special discounts for sales promotion, corporate gifts, fund-raising, or educational purposes. Special editions can also be created to specifications. For details, contact the Special Sales Department, Skyhorse Publishing, 307 West 36th Street, 11th Floor, New York, NY 10018 or info@skyhorsepublishing.com.

Racehorse Publishing™ is a pending trademark of Skyhorse Publishing, Inc.®, a Delaware corporation.

Visit our website at www.skyhorsepublishing.com.

10 9 8 7 6 5 4 3 2

Library of Congress Cataloging-in-Publication Data is available on file.

Cover design by Brian Peterson
Cover artwork Getty Images

Print ISBN: 978-1-63158-643-9
Ebook ISBN: 978-1-63158-652-1

Printed in China

CONTENTS

INTRODUCTION

TIKTOK WHAT?

Yes, you know what TikTok is, and you may even feel like a book of TikTok tips is counterintuitive. But hold on a minute. TikTok may look like a simple app for sharing and watching videos, but looks can be deceiving. There is a whole lot to unlock within this platform, and this book helps you take advantage of all you can do with it. Even though there are websites, videos, and TikTok communities devoted to giving you tips and hacks to what is now the sixth most popular social media destination and the most downloaded app, we felt there was a need to provide a static and steady place to read, learn, and go more in depth than the other aforementioned destinations. We did research! We read the articles and watched the videos! We played with the video effects! We spent countless hours on TikTok scrolling and, most importantly, taking notes. What follows is what we've discovered. (By the way, "we" are myself and my dog, Rooster. For the purposes of this book, we've created a TikTok account featuring Rooster, whose only goal in life is to achieve fame.) A lot of what you learn about TikTok is through trial and error, and that's fine, but we've taken out a lot of the guesswork as we cover the basics and also delve into the less obvious tips and hacks that will help you be where you want to be with this app.

From getting started with TikTok to getting famous, the tips in this book provide just what you need, whether you're posting videos two to three times a day in order to become an influencer, trying to get likes and followers, or simply in it for some fun.

A BIT ABOUT TIKTOK

Much like its predecessors, Vine, Dubsmash, and Musical. ly, TikTok is an app (iOS and Android) with which users can create and share short-form mobile videos. That means, using only our smartphones, we can shoot videos from five to sixty seconds long, edit them on the phone, add song clips or original sounds, and post them on the app. No special cameras needed. No video-editing software required. No advanced degrees warranted. Just you, your smartphone, and your ideas. If you're joining TikTok just to watch videos, that's fine, too!

TikTok has been around since September 2017. It started off as an offshoot of the Chinese platform known as Douyin, which launched in China the previous year. Douyin and TikTok are basically the same app, but they are run on different networks in order to comply with Chinese censorship restrictions. In November 2017, TikTok's parent company, ByteDance, dropped around $1 billion to acquire Musical.ly. At that time, Musical.ly had around 100 million users. In August 2018, TikTok and Musical.ly merged with all existing Musical.ly accounts transferred over to TikTok.

Today, TikTok is the fastest-growing social media platform in the world. As we write this, TikTok:

- is available in 154 countries
- has been downloaded more than 130 million times in the US and 1.5 billion times worldwide

- has 1 billion users worldwide
- has 800 million monthly active users

It is also estimated that TikTok users spend an average of about one hour a day on the platform and open the app eight times a day.

As for who is using the app:

- 60 percent are between the ages of 16 to 24
- 26 percent are between the ages 25 to 44
- 80 percent are between the ages 16 to 34

TikTok is growing fast with no end in sight. While it may seem daunting entering such a crowded field of lip-syncers, dancers, gymnasts, comedians, and more, there is definitely room for you in this content heavy environment. Read on to get started!

WHAT YOU CAN DO ON TIKTOK

The tips in this book are separated by the different things you can do on TikTok.

Chapter 1: Signing Up

This is pretty self-explanatory. We take you through setting up your profile and helpfully pointing out what all the icons and words on your Home screen mean.

Chapter 2: Watching Videos

TikTok users don't just create videos—they watch them! This chapter helps you discover the content you want to see and hide the stuff that bothers you.

Chapter 3: Making Movies

Now, this is where the magic happens! You get to make your own videos. These tips will help you make your videos look good and make an impression.

Chapter 4: Interacting

Even more than the videos, TikTok is all about members of a community communicating and interacting with one another. Users can follow accounts they like, give videos hearts (likes), gifts, comments, and more.

Chapter 5: Going Viral

There are no guarantees in life . . . and with TikTok, breaking through with a viral video can be a daunting task. This chapter takes away as much of the guesswork as possible.

Chapter 6: Taking Care of Yourself

This chapter gives you advice on making sure you're protecting your identity and yourself as you are putting yourself and your videos out there.

CHAPTER 1
SIGNING UP

Ready to sign up? Here are the steps to take. Every now and then TikTok updates the interface; however, the steps for signing up for an account don't usually change.

Once you've downloaded the app, the first screen will ask you to Choose Your Interests. You can tap on specific interests you have or skip this screen altogether. If you know you are interested in a few different categories of videos you want to shoot at some point, go ahead and tap on those categories. Otherwise, skip this step.

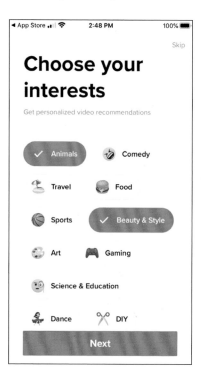

1. Choose as many as you want or skip this step altogether. (It doesn't seem to matter, because TikTok has got you covered as it bases what videos you see on what you watch.)

2. The very next screen tells you what to do next! Pretty simple!

READY TO SIGN UP?

Tap on the **Me** icon in the lower right-hand corner of the screen. Tap the red **Sign up** box.

1. You can sign up using your phone number or email or through Facebook, Google, an Apple device, Twitter, Instagram, or Android device. Tap on the small arrow indicated below to see all of your options. Choose any method you want, but remember which you choose in case you want to create more than one account (see Tip #105 on page 122).

2. Give them your birthday ... or *a* birthday. You have to be over thirteen to open a TikTok account, and TikTok regularly deletes accounts if the user is under that age. Just know that once you enter a birthday, you can't change it. Tap **Continue** when you're done.

3. Enter your valid phone number or email in order to receive a verification code to continue.

4. Type in the code. You will be directed to a simple Captcha to confirm you are a human.

5. Create your password.

It has to be at least eight characters (and up to twenty). You must include two of the following: letters, numbers, and/ or special characters.

6. Create your username (see Tip #115 on page 134). Your username has to be unique—meaning no one else on TikTok can share the same username as you. If the username you choose is already taken, you will get a note saying, "This username has been taken. Please try a different one."

That's it. You're signed up and ready to make some magic.

FILL IN THE BLANKS

Well, before the magic, there is still a little more housekeeping to take care of. You can change your assigned TikTok name, add a short bio, add a profile pic or video, and more!

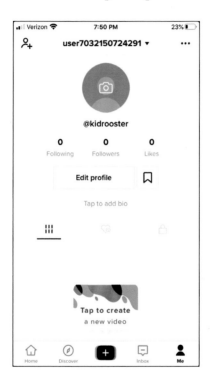

This is your **Profile** screen. You get to it by tapping on the **Me** icon at the bottom right-hand corner of the screen. Tap on **Edit profile** in order to change your TikTok assigned name, add biography info, add Instagram, and/or YouTube. This is also where you can add a profile photo or video. This is what your followers will see when they go to check you out, so you want it to look awesome.

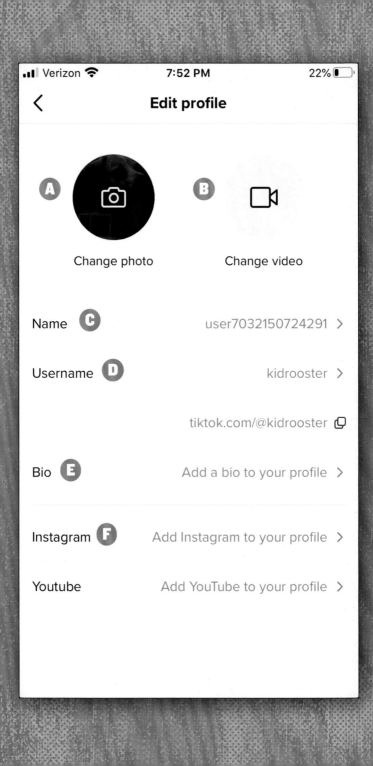

A. Tap here to access photos on your phone. Choose one for your profile pic. Or better yet, take a new one, but take a shower first—you want to look your best!

B. You can decide to use a six-second video clip instead of a photo. Start by tapping here. (More on creating videos on page 52.)

C. TikTok auto-generates a name for you. Change it by tapping here. The Name appears at the top of your page. Don't skip this step. Nothing looks worse than your name, "user7032150724291" showing up instead of the cool one that's still in your head.

D. This is your TikTok username that you created already. This is your handle. Click on the 2-square icon to copy a link that will take anyone right to your Profile screen.

E. Add your bio here. (See page 137 for more on bios.)

F. Tapping either of these will take you to their sign-ins. Type in your username and password to link your accounts.

TIP #1

Save Your Work

Whenever you are changing anything in your profile, make sure to find and tap **Save**. It's easy to miss (even though it is red!), and if you do, you have to start over.

TIP #2

Complete Your Profile

Your profile is your first impression. It is who you are on TikTok—your personality or brand, so to speak—so think about what you want to say about yourself as you fill in the blanks as precisely as possible. You want your visitors to "get" who you are quickly. So, decide what category or niche you are going to own and be consistent about it throughout your profile creation. Are you a lip-syncer, a dancer, a comedian, a prankster, or an observer of life? It helps if you know what you're going to do on TikTok before you fill in the blanks. As you'll find out later, being on TikTok isn't so much about being original as it is about bringing a new voice to everything that's already out there. So, don't reinvent the wheel, but instead, polish the wheel with your own particular glow.

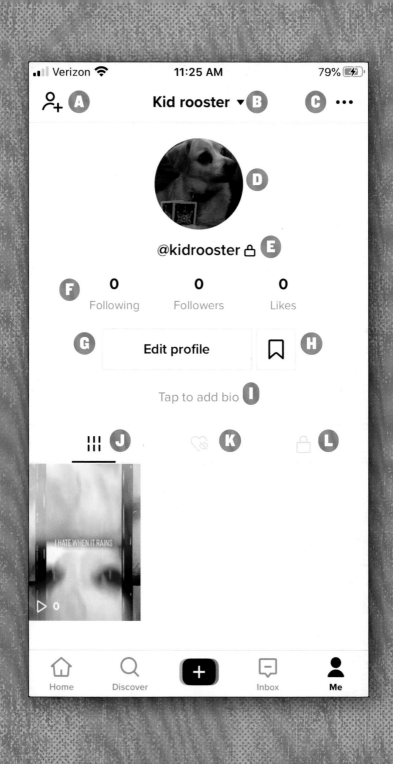

YOUR PROFILE SCREEN (A.K.A. ME PAGE)

A. Leads to three options: inviting friends, finding contacts, and finding Facebook friends. (See Tip #86 on page 103 for more.)

B. Your name. Tapping on this takes you to where you can add an account. (See Tip #105 on page 122 for more.)

C. Takes you to your Privacy and settings page.

D. Your profile video or photograph.

E. Tapping on this copies your username to your phone's clipboard.

F. Your stat line. It will look sad when you're just starting out.

G. To edit your profile, obviously.

H. This takes you to your liked videos, hashtags, sounds, and effects.

I. This is where your biography appears. You only have 80 characters to play with, so make your words count.

J. The videos you've created.

K. The videos you've liked.

L. The videos you've created that only you can view. (See Chapter 6: Taking Care of Yourself for more on privacy.)

TIP #3

Privacy and Settings

From your Profile page, tap on the **More (. . .)** icon at the top right-hand corner of your screen. This takes you to your **Privacy and settings** screen. From here you can make changes to your account as well as report a problem, get help, read TikTok's terms of use, and more. See **Chapter 6: Taking Care of Yourself** for more on these settings.

TIP #4

Know What You're Talking About

There is a certain amount of TikTok slang that is good to be familiar with as you begin playing around on the app.

Challenges: Challenges are a big deal on TikTok! A challenge is a format for a video in which everyone pretty much does the same thing . . . but with their own twist on it. One example of a challenge is to mimic a series of dance moves to a specific song. One famous Challenge is the Flip the Switch in which two people (usually a man and a woman) dance in the bathroom. They turn off the light, and when they turn it back on, they have switched clothing . . . all set to Drake's "Nonstop."

Comments: These are the notes you leave on other people's videos and that you receive from people watching yours. These can be filtered or disabled (see Tip #90 on page 107).

Community: TikTok calls its users a community because it encourages its users to come together "to create, share, and inspire."

Creator: Anyone who posts a video on TikTok is considered a creator.

Duets: This feature allows a creator to collaborate with another user's video. The two videos are then side-by-side. For example, the original video can be a person dancing crazily with their elbow flailing. The duet can feature a user's cereal tipping over when an elbow flails in that direction. In other instances, users film themselves dancing the same dance as the original. Users can control who can and cannot duet with their videos (see Tip #95 on page 113).

Fans: Once you follow a TikTok user's profile, you become their fan.

"For You" Page: This can be found on your Home page and is the place where new videos are recommended to you based on the users, creators, and videos you already like or view frequently.

Hashtag: This is a tag used on many social networks that helps other users easily find videos. For instance, if looking for videos of dancing dogs, you could search #dancingdogs.

Hearts: Tapping on the **Heart** icon means you liked a user's video.

Private Messaging: This allows you to talk to another user privately. You can also exchange videos privately with this function. You are in control of who can chat with you (See page 170.)

Profile: This is what you call the information you have provided about yourself that shows up on your **Profile** page (**Me** icon).

Reactions: This function allows users to respond to videos by showing how they feel about them. As with **Duets**, this function also requires a user's permission.

Report: This function helps maintain a positive community and TikTok experience. Users are encouraged to report user profiles, videos, chats, and content that contain harassment, offensive behavior/comments, or inappropriate content that causes discomfort.

TIP #5

Is One Phone Better Than Another?

Like with anything else, the more you spend, the more you get. You're going to want a phone with a big screen, good battery life, and an amazing camera. If you have the cash on hand for the latest iPhone or Samsung Galaxy Note, that's great. Whether you're operating in iOS or Android, you'll have no problems. A good alternative for budget-conscious users is the OnePlus 7T, which has an amazing camera, or the Infinix Hot 8, which has a triple rear camera that includes three sensors and a super long-lasting battery. Overall, though, most of today's top phones are going to be fine for what you're doing on TikTok, so don't feel bad if you don't have the latest brand or model. Start with what you have and take it from there. And if you can, have a backup phone (perhaps your old phone if you didn't trade it in), just in case of accidents.

CHAPTER 2
WATCHING VIDEOS

Some TikTok users are perfectly happy just watching videos without ever thinking about filming something themselves. Whether you're looking for followers or just something to make you laugh, this chapter will help you make the most out of your viewing.

ALL THOSE ICONS

On your **Home** page, there's a lot going on besides the video you're watching. There are words at the top of the page and icons on the bottom and along the right side of the page. Also, you can see the video creator's tag, whatever hashtags they've assigned to their video, and what sound they are using for the video.

Navigation at the top of the Home Page

Following: Go here to see videos from people you are following.
For You: This is where you see videos from people you aren't following. TikTok sends you a mix of popular content, new content, and content based on videos you watch.

Words in the Lower Left-hand Corner of the Home Page

A. Creator's handle

B. Creator's video description

C. Hashtags used to help find and categorize the video (more on hashtags on page 45).

D. Name of the sound (song clip) being used in the video (more on sounds on page 63)

Navigation Buttons Along the Right Side

E. This takes you to the profile of the creator you're watching. Tap to go to their Profile page or long press until the + symbol disappears. This means you're now following this user.

F. Tap the Heart icon to like the video you're watching.

G. This is the Comment icon. Tap on it to read and make comments on the current video.

H. The Share icon lets you share the current video with friends you may already have on TikTok as well as to other social media platforms. There are also tools for saving, reporting, and more.

I. This spinning disk takes you to the music or sound currently playing along with the video. Tap on this to see other videos using the same sound.

Navigation Buttons at the Bottom of the Home Page

Home: This takes you to your **Home** page, which is where you are right now!

Discover: This opens up collections of popular videos grouped by trending hashtags.

+ sign (Upload): Tap to open the **Record** page. Here you can film a video, edit it, add filters, and more . . . once you have an account.

Inbox: Here you can read messages from other users to the creator of the video you are watching.

Me: This takes you to your **Profile** page.

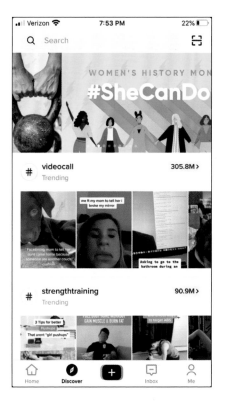

This is what the **Discover** page looks like.

TIP #6

Type in Search Items

From the **Discover** page you can also search for videos, sounds, users, and hashtags by typing in terms at the top of the page.

TIP #7

Use the Scan Icon

Another feature of the **Discover** page is the **Scan** icon [−] in the top right-hand corner, which opens up a viewfinder to capture someone's TikCode.

I. Tap the **Scan** icon [–] in the top right-hand corner of the screen. This opens a viewfinder that works like a QR code that takes you directly to the TikCode's user's **Profile** page. (More on TikCodes on page 117).

TIPS FOR WATCHING

Here are a bunch of tips for getting the most out of your viewing experience.

TIP #8

You Don't Need an Account

You may decide to begin your TikTok research by simply watching a ton of videos. That's easy. Download the app onto your smartphone, skip the whole creating a profile thing for now, and follow the directions! What you're able to do on the app is limited, but you can watch videos as you please. However, you can't comment on videos, follow anyone, like videos, and most importantly for some folks, create videos!

TIP #9

Use Your Computer

Another way to watch TikTok videos without an account is to use your desktop or laptop computer.

1. Go to tiktok.com and click on the red **Watch now** button. You can watch **Trending** videos, or if you click on the three lines in the upper left-hand corner of the site, you can choose **Discover**, which will take you to the latest trending videos as well as trending hashtags.

This is a great way to experience TikTok for the first time . . . after that, you're going to want to set up an account on your phone!

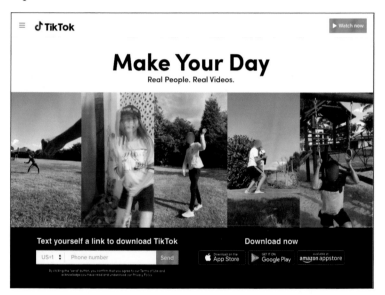

TIP #10

Swipe Away

TikTok uses their top-secret algorithm to begin figuring out what type of content you want by what you watch. The more you watch, the better TikTok gets at predicting what you like. If you get tired of a certain theme or type of content, keep swiping before the videos play all the way through, and you'll begin to see fewer and fewer of these types of videos. TikTok is watching you watch.

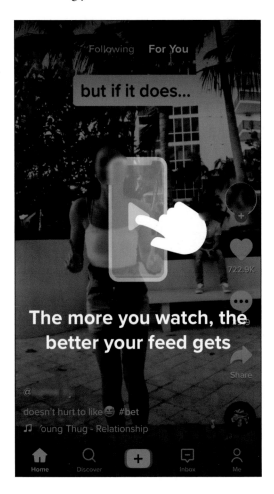

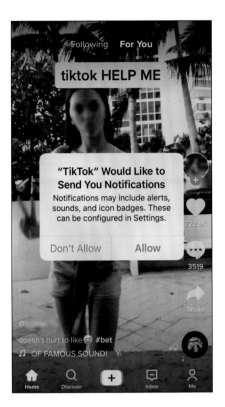

You can also decide at this time what kinds of push notifications you want. Tap **Allow** for what types of notifications you'd like to utilize. See page 168 for more.

TIP #11

Finger Gestures for Maneuvering

- To pause the video: Tap the main part of the screen once. Make sure to tap anywhere on the video that is not covered up with hashtags or icons. Tap again to play the video.

- To scroll through videos: Swipe up or down.
- Swipe to the left: This toggles the **Profile** page for the creator of the video you're watching.

TIP #12

Double Tap Trick

Tapping your finger twice on the video likes it. Some videos will have an inserted image somewhere that pops up for a fraction of a second. It's done supposedly to test your pausing skills; however, it often gets you to tap quickly enough to inadvertently like it. Other videos promise a punchline or answer if you double tap the video or press the + button, which of course, means you just followed them. Pretty sneaky.

TIP #13

Quick Actions

Long press for TikTok Quick Actions. Holding your finger on a video takes you to more options, which include:

- **Not interested**: Tap this if you don't like the video and don't wish to see more like this.
- **Save video**: This saves the video to your phone's **Photos** for ease of access. In other words, you're downloading it.
- **Add to Favorites**: Tap this and the video is saved to your **Favorites** page, which only shows up if you have an account.

- If you tap **More**, you get:
  - ▸ **Hide videos from this user**: So you no longer have to watch videos from a particular person.
  - ▸ **Hide videos with this sound:** If you can't stand the song clip that's being used.

TIP #14

Check Out the Most Followed Accounts

TikRank.com keeps an updated list of

- The top TikTok Influencers
- The Most Viewed Videos
- The Most Popular Hashtags
- And more!

TIP #15

Check Out the Popular Creators

When just starting out, it is worth it to check out the popular creators. These are video uploaders who have at least 100,000 followers and active fans. To check out these folks, tap **Following** at the top of the **Home** page. This will take you to TikTok's curated list of **Trending Creators**. Yes, there are a lot of famous people's accounts, but it's still worth checking them out! And if you like what you see, tap **Follow.** Once you are following accounts, you'll see videos from these users instead of the Trending Creators page.

TIP #16

See (or Hear) Something You Don't Like?

You can easily tell TikTok to stop sending you videos or trends you don't like.

1. As you're watching a video, press and hold your finger on the video.

2. Tap **Not interested**. This will let TikTok know you're not interested in certain trends or simply videos in the same vein. For instance, if you don't like cats, tell TikTok you're not interested in the next cat video you see, and you will see fewer of them.

41

3. You can also access **Not interested** from the **Share** icon. Tap **Share** and find the **Not interested** button. Tap it and you will be directed away from the video immediately!

TIP #17

How to Find Videos Featuring Sounds You Like

To find videos using an audio clip (sound) you like, do the following:

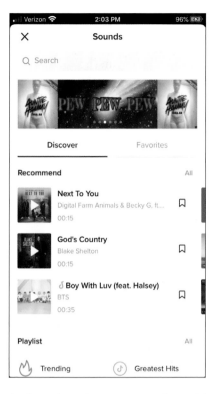

1. Once you find a video playing a sound you like, tap the **spinning circle** (record) at the bottom of the right-side menu bar. Or . . . tap the scrolling **sound link** at the bottom of the video. They both take you to the same place.

2. You're now at the sound's page. From here you can add the sound to your **Favorites**, share it, find the original video that first used the sound, and view every video that uses the sound. (If it's a popular song, there could be millions of videos.)

3. Tap the **Use this sound** button to record a video using the sound.

TIP #18

Search and Find TikTok Videos by Cool Effects

If you get to a video that has a box above the creator's handle with a wand, that is the effect used in the video. (More on effects on page 55.)

1. Tap the name of the effect to go to that effect's page.

2. From there you can add the effect to your favorites, share the effect, and find all the videos that use it.

3. Tap on the red button if you want to record a video using the effect.

TIP #19

Search and Find TikTok Videos by Hashtags

Want to see more videos tagged with a particular hashtag, like #FYP?

1. Find and watch a video with the hashtag.

2. Tap the hashtag. It appears in the video's caption, below the creator's handle.

3. From the hashtag's page that pops up, you can add the hashtag to your favorites, share it, and find every video tagged with that hashtag. You can even start recording a new video to tag.

4. You can also find hashtags from your **Discover** page. From the **Home** page, tap **Discover**. There you will find trending hashtags.

TIP #20

Add a TikTok Video to Your Favorites

Adding a video to your favorites makes it really easy to find again to watch whenever you want. It looks like a bookmark, because that's essentially what you're doing here!

1. When you find a video you want to favorite, tap the **Share** button (the arrow) on the right-hand side of the page. Please note, if the creator doesn't allow saving or sharing, you won't be able to do this.

2. Tap **Add to Favorites**.

TIP #21

Watch Your Favorites

Head to your **Favorites** when you're looking for inspiration or you want to share something with a friend.

1. Tap the **Me** icon to go to your **Profile** page.

2. Tap the **Bookmark** icon next to the **Edit profile** button.

3. You'll find your favorites separated by **Videos**, **Hashtags**, **Sounds**, and **Effects**.

TIP #22

Share a TikTok Video

If you find a video you want to share with friends, if the creator allows it, you can share several different ways.

1. Tap the **Share** icon (the arrow). If the creator doesn't allow sharing, this icon isn't visible. Some creators allow you to share their videos.

2. Tap where you want to share the video: Text message, Snapchat, Instagram, Instagram Stories, Facebook Messenger, Facebook, Twitter, WhatsApp, and email.

3. You can also tap the **Links** button to copy a link to the video, which you can then paste where you want it.

4. If you tap the **Other** button, it takes you to your phone's share page, where it might be easier for you to text it to someone specific.

TIP #23

Save a TikTok Video

1. Tap the **Share** icon (the arrow). If the creator doesn't allow saving, you won't see this icon.

2. Hit the **Save** icon. The video is now saved to your phone's photo library.

TIP #24

Create a Live Photo from a TikTok Video

Another way to enjoy TikTok videos is to turn a video into a **Live Photo**, which you can then use on your lock screen.

I. This is easiest on an iPhone that has 3-D Touch. Tap the **Share** icon (the arrow).

2. Tap the **Live Photo** button on the second row. If you don't see the icon, the creator doesn't allow sharing.

3. Then save the video as a Live Photo in your Photos on your phone. Find it and set it up as your wallpaper for your lock screen. (It only works on the lock screen . . . not your home screen background.

4. For Android devices, you'll have to first install the TikTok All Picture app first.

TIP #25

Create a GIF from a TikTok Video

You can also convert a TikTok into a GIF you can share or save to your Photos. You can share the GIF, but know that It'll be watermarked.

I. Tap the **Share** icon (the arrow).

2. Tap the **Share as GIF** icon in the second row.

3. The video will be turned into a GIF, which you will

then be prompted to share via text, Facebook Messenger, WhatsApp, Twitter, and more.

4. If you don't want to share it just yet (or at all), tap **Done**. The GIF will appear in your photo library.

CHAPTER 3
MAKING MOVIES

Shooting videos is fun . . . and ultimately the very reason you joined TikTok in the first place! TikTok's mission is to inspire creativity and bring joy, and yes, that's part of the reason you might want to create videos on this platform. This chapter covers the nuts and bolts of creating videos that inspire your creativity while bringing joy, but it also provides tips and tricks for getting your videos liked and you followed.

When shooting and editing your video, you'll encounter three different pages.

1. The Camera Page: This is where you set your preferences and record your video clips.

2. The Preview Page: This is where you view what you recorded and edit until you're happy.

3. The Post Page: This is where you set your posting preferences, add a description about the video, and send it out to the TikTok world.

TIP #26

Answer This One Question

We hinted at this earlier, but before you start shooting, decide *why* you want to be on TikTok. What is it about your personality are you wishing to showcase? What's your brand or theme? Are you going to be cringy and humiliate yourself on purpose? Are you a basketball player who wants to show off your moves while commenting on the NBA? Do you want to dance, lip-sync, tell jokes, do science experiments? Who do you think will want to watch your content? Figure this out before you begin shooting videos because deciding on a niche is a very important way of getting people to follow you.

THE CAMERA PAGE

From your **Home** page, tap the + button in the bottom middle of the screen. This takes you to where you can shoot videos. As with the other pages on TikTok, there is a lot going on here. But essentially, at any time, you can press the big red button in the bottom middle of the page to start filming. Press the smaller red square to stop.

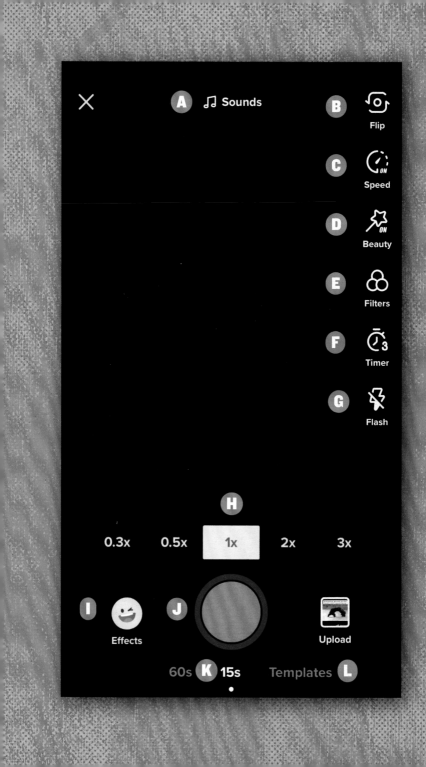

A. Tap here to access sounds.

B. Tap here to flip your phone's camera.

C. Tap here to turn on or off the speed controls.

D. Tap here for beauty mode.

E. Tap here for different filters you can apply to your video.

F. Tap the timer to set a countdown for beginning the video as well as for ending it.

G. This turns on or off your phone's flash.

H. Tap here to control recording speed.

I. Tap here to access the hundreds of different effects that you can use on your videos.

J. This big red button is for, you guessed it, shooting your video.

K. Decide whether you want a 15-second video or up to a 60-second video.

L. Templates are for creating videos with photos.

TIP #27

Adjust Your Recording Preferences Before You Shoot

Before you shoot, figure out your preferences on the **Camera** page. This is the point in the creative process where you decide whether or not to enable beauty mode, what affects you want to use, what filters you want to add, and what speed you want to film at. Shoot a few videos playing around with the settings before you publish them.

TIP #28

Edit on the Camera Page

While you can add effects after shooting in the **Preview** page, there's more functionality pre-production than post production. Think of the **Preview** page as post-production tinkering and not the place to start thinking about effects and filters.

TIP #29

More Tips on Filming

While some videos are one take—a dance, for example—many are filmed by combining several clips within one recording session. Within each segment or clip, you can change filters, effects, and more. You can also change the perspective of the video. If you're filming two people talking to each other close up, you can stop recording the first person to then focus on the second one. The best way to get a handle on how to do this effectively is to watch videos that utilize different effects throughout the video or shoot from different angles within one video. The more you practice this, the better you will get.

TIP #30

Select the Length of Your Video

1. Look for the faded "60s" and "15s" at the bottom of the page.

2. 60s means you have up to 60 seconds to film. 15s means you have up to 15 seconds.

3. Tap whichever one you wish to use.

TIP #31

How Long Should Your Videos Be?

When first starting out, always make your videos 15 seconds. TikTok is a short-attention-span environment, and if you want people to watch your videos all the way through, it pays to make them short. TikTok rewards videos that are played all the way through and more than once. Spend some time watching TikTok videos. How many times do you swipe up on a video that goes on longer than 15 seconds?

TIP #32

Change the Speed of your TikTok Video

1. If you don't see a row with the numbers 0.3x, 0.5x, 1x, 2x, and 3x, tap on the Speed icon on the right side of the page. The row should pop up.

2. 1x is normal speed.

3. .3x and .5x are for slow motion.

4. 2x and 3x are for fast motion.

TIP #33

What Are Fast and Slow Motion Good For?

Sports highlights, pratfalls, facial expressions, dance moves, etc.

TIP #34

Experiment with Effects

1. Set up the phone near your face.

2. Make sure to flip the phone's camera so you are in selfie mode.

3. Tap **Effects**.

4. Try out the different effects on you! You can try effects that are **Trending**, **New**, and in several other categories.

TIP #35

Add an Effect to Your TikTok Video

From adding disco lights to making your video look old fashioned, you can spend all day experimenting with the effects and not get to them all.

1. Tap the **Effect** button on the right of the **Camera** page.

2. Find and tap on an effect you wish to use.

3. You can add more effects later on the **Preview** page.

4. Tap on the screen once you're done to return to the **Camera** page.

TIP #36

Bookmark an Effect

If you see an effect you like and may want to use often or later on, do the following:

1. Tap on the effect for the **Camera** page.

2. As you see the preview of the effect on the screen, tap on the bookmark icon in the middle left of the page.

3. Now, whenever you go to **Effects**, you can tap on the bookmark just before the word **Trending** to find your favs.

TIP #37

Using Green Screen . . . No Actual Green Screen Required!!!

The **Green Screen** effect has quickly become one of TikTok's most used effects. With a few adjustments, you go from being in your bedroom to standing in front of the Eiffel Tower or in a grocery cart. As TikTok says, "the best part is—there's no actual green screen or suit with ping pong balls required." To use the **Green Screen** effect, follow these simple instructions:

1. Select **Effects** and under the **Trending** section, look for the **#greenscreen** icon. It looks like this:

2. Choose any photo from your phone's library to use your background and tap **Record**!

3. You can also easily create a video featuring you visiting the sites of the world!

4. Collect photos you have (or free photos online that are in the public domain) and make sure they are in your phone's photos.

5. Choose your first **Green Screen** image. Pose yourself as if interacting with the image. For instance, you can be giving the Statue of Liberty a high five.

6. Set the timer for this clip (see Tip #49 on page 68).

7. Tap **Record** and get into position.

8. When the clip is recorded, use the **Green Screen** effects again for the next clip and choose another image to be your background. Repeat until your video is done.

TIP #38

Add a Filter to Your TikTok Video

1. Tap the **Filters** icon on the right of the screen.

2. Choose how you want to change the look of your video and tap on that filter.

3. You can also swipe to the left to run through all the filters while previewing how they will make your video look.

4. Tap on the screen once you're done to return to the **Camera** page.

TIP #39

Experiment with Filters

1. Set up your phone in a place with good lighting.

2. Tap **Filters** on the right of the page.

3. The filters are separated by these groups: **Portrait**, **Landscape**, **Food**, and **Vibe**.

4. Play around a bit to see which filters you like.

TIP #40

Get Rid of Unwanted Filters

1. Tap on **Management**.

2. From there you can scroll through the filters and tap on the brighter checkmarks to remove the ones you don't want to see.

3. The darker checkmarks cannot be tapped. These filters will always show up.

TIP #41

Add a Sound to Your TikTok Video

Music is an essential part of the TikTok experience. There are countless song snippets you can use for your videos.

1. Tap the **Sounds** link at the top of the **Camera** page. This will take you to the **Sounds** page. From here you can search or browse thousands of song snippets, including samples from top pop stars.

2. If you know the sound you want, search for it by typing it into the **Search** bar at the top of the page.

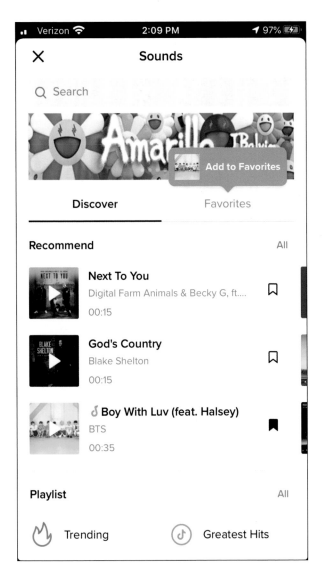

3. You can also explore through the **Discover** tab or by tapping on the categories in the **Playlist** area.

4. Below the **Playlist** area are songs separated by genre.

5. Tap on the song you want to use, and then tap on the checkmark that appears.

6. When recording, the sound will begin as soon as you tap on the record button.

TIP #42

How to Favorite a Sound

1. If you find a song you like, you can add it to your favorites by tapping on the **Bookmark** icon next to the song's title.

2. These songs now appear in the **Favorites** tab on the **Sounds** page as well as on your **Favorites** page, which you access from your **Profile** page.

TIP #43

Add a Beauty Filter to Your TikTok Video

When creating a TikTok, tap the **Beauty** button on the right of the **Camera** page to subtly clean up your face.

1. Tap **Beauty** on the right side of the **Camera** page.

2. Some find this effect can sometimes make your face look a little fake. Others, however, swear by it.

TIP #44

What Are Templates?

If you want to showcase a few photos instead of shooting a video, you can tap **Templates** and choose one of about ten different ways to do your slideshow. **Morph** is a pretty popular effect that morphs faces from one photo to another.

TIP #45

Keep Everything in Focus

To make sure the object you want to film is in focus, tap on the object on the **Camera** page. A white circle will appear, which then resets the camera's focus, if needed.

TIP #46

Get a Little Closer

If you want to zoom in on the action, place two fingers close together on the screen and un-pinch them to zoom in. Pinch the fingers to zoom out.

TIP #47

Use a Video That Already Exists

Maybe you want to use a video you took on your phone a while back.

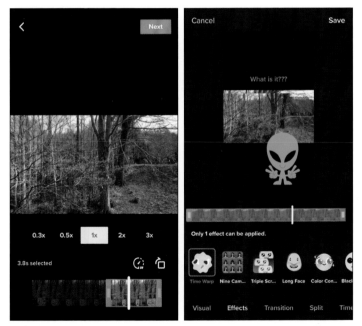

1. Tap the **Upload** icon. That will take you to your phone's saved photos and videos.

2. Select what you want to use and then tap **Next**.

3. Here you can edit the video. You can shorten it either at the beginning or end by moving the red lines at either side of the video.

4. You can also change the speed at which it plays by tapping the timer icon.

5. Tap the rotate icon to rotate the video.

6. When you're done, tap **Next** to apply a sound, an effect, text, and stickers.

TIP #48

Get a Dash Cam

If you're looking for something interesting to post, try using a dash cam for your car or a camera you can affix to your bike helmet. Sooner or later you'll get something interesting to post!

TIP #49

Set the Timer

If you need a slight delay before you start filming, tap the **Timer** icon.

I. Choose either 3s or 10s (if you need more time to get ready).

TIP #50

Setting the Timer for Stopping

This function is great if you're not manning the phone and you only want to record a shorter clip for a longer video.

1. To choose a stop time, place your finger on the red line with the red dot on top of it and scroll it to the left to the desired stop time.

2. When you're ready to shoot, tap **Start countdown.**

(Do this step only after you've set up all of your other preferences as your only choice here is to Start countdown!)

3. This function is great for when you know you want to film for an exact number of seconds. For instance, if you want a five-second clip of you dancing, move the red line until it says 5.0 seconds. Tap **Start countdown**, get in front of the phone, and dance. The video stops recording at five seconds without you having to press the stop recording button. This comes in handy when you're doing transitions.

TIP #51

The Type of Video You Want Dictates How You Record It

There are a few different ways to shoot your videos.

1. One Clip: In some cases, you will want to set up your phone, set the timer, get in front of the phone, and shoot 15 seconds in one take. In that case, you set your timer, press record, and wait for the time to run out.

2. Many Clips: If you are "manning" the phone while filming, you can tap the record button and then tap again to stop.

3. Many Clips: Press and hold the record button. Let go of the button when you want to stop recording. This is great for really quick takes.

4. Recording for a set length of time.

And . . . Action!

After all your preferences are set, you're ready to record!

1. Tap the red button to record.

2. When ready to stop recording, tap the red square. Alternatively, if you're shooting just one take, you can let the time run out (15 seconds or 60 seconds). Or, use the press and hold method described above.

Note: The **Camera** page will automatically stop recording once you run out of time.

3. Whether you are shooting several clips or just one long shot, you will automatically be taken to the **Preview** page only after you use up your allotted time.

4. If you like the clip you created, tap the white checkmark in the red circle.

5. If you want to delete the clip, tap the **X** in the white polygon.

6. After shooting a whole video or a clip, and you tap on the checkmark, you will be taken to the **Preview** page (see page 73) where your video plays on a loop. From here you can make further edits.

7. Tap **Next** from the **Preview** page if you're happy with what you have. This takes you to the **Post** page (see page 91). Here you can add hashtags and adjust who can view, comment, duet and react, and save to their device.

TIP #52

Unhappy with Your Video?

1. Tap the **X** in the top left-hand corner of the **Camera** page. From here you can choose **Reshoot**, **Exit**, or **Cancel**. **Exit** takes you out of shooting mode and deletes your work. **Cancel** returns you to the page.

TIP #53

Zoom In and Out While Recording

While shooting a clip, there are two ways to zoom in and out on a subject.

1. Using the press and hold method of recording, you can zoom in on your subject while holding the record button. Move your finger toward the center of the page and the camera will zoom in. To zoom back out, move your finger that's holding the record button back toward the bottom of the page.

2. If you're press-and-release recording use your finger on the page to pinch open and pinch close to zoom in and out.

THE PREVIEW PAGE

You shot your video . . . now what? TikTok takes you to a **Preview** page where your video plays on a loop. From here you can add and position text; edit or change your **Sound**, **Effects**, and **Filters**; add **stickers** or **emojis;** and more. More details are on pages 75–90.

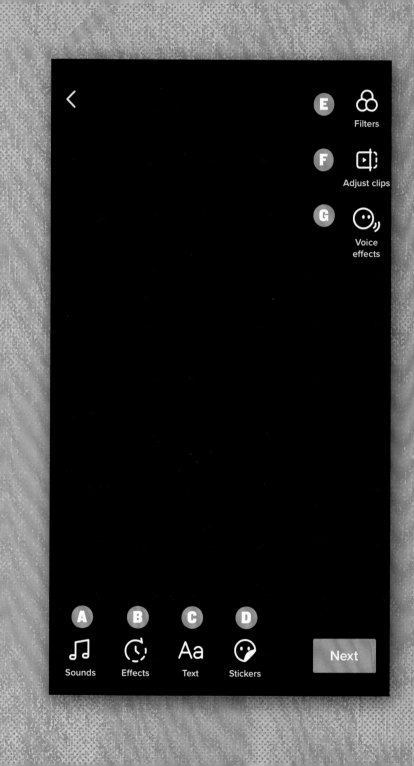

A. You can add your soundtrack after shooting.

B. Forgot your effects? Do it now!

C. This is where you can add text for context.

D. From here you can add stickers or emojis to your video.

E. Add filters!

F. If you shot your video with several different clips, you can edit and adjust them here.

G. Want to sound like a chipmunk? You've come to the right place.

TIP #54

Return to Camera Page

Want to keep recording? That's fine, but all your edits on the **Preview** page will be deleted! Also, do not exit TikTok from the **Preview** page. You might lose all your work. Simply tap **Next** and then the **Drafts** button at the bottom of the **Post** page.

TIP #55

Adjust Your Clips From the Preview Page

This allows you to move your clips around and shorten them.

1. Whatever you do, ADJUST YOUR CLIPS first! If you don't you will lose all the editing you do.

2. From the **Adjust Clips** page, you will see your clips at the bottom of the page. Long press one of the clips to move it somewhere else. This will automatically reorder your video.

3. Tap on one of the clips to edit it.

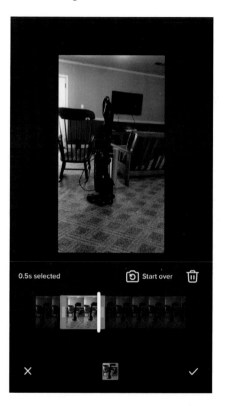

4. From here you can move the red bars to edit its length. You can also tap **Reshoot** if you don't like what you're seeing. Tap the trash can to delete this clip.

5. Don't forget to tap **Save** when you're done!

TIP #56

Adding Filters from the Preview Page

1. Filters work the same way as they do on the **Camera** page. See page 62.

2. Remember you can swipe left or right to preview the different filters.

3. Once you select a filter you want to use, tap it. Then tap the video to return to the **Preview** page.

TIP #57

Adding Sound from the Preview Page

Selecting your sounds before shooting for lip-syncing and dancing is essential. In other cases, you may wish to wait until the **Preview** page to add your sound.

1. Tap on **Sounds**. From here you can tap on **Soundtrack** and select the song snippet you want.

TIP #58

Adjust the Volume of Original Sound and Soundtrack

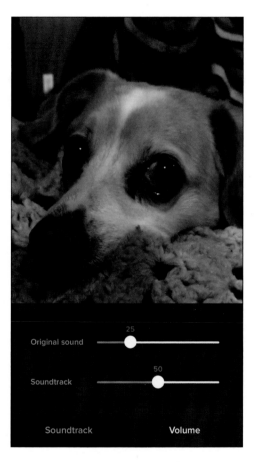

1. Tap **Volume** after selecting your Sound.

2. Move the volume button to the left or right to adjust either the **Original sound** or the **Soundtrack**.

TIP #59

Adjust Sound Positioning

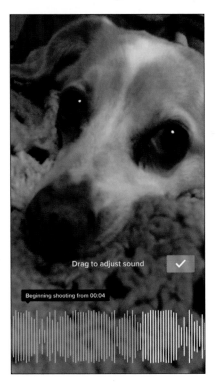

You can adjust where in the song you wish to begin.

1. Tap on the musical notes with the little scissors.

2. While the video loops you can move the song until you're happy with where it is.

3. Don't forget to tap the checkmark when you are done.

4. By the way, this works with **Sounds** chosen either from the **Camera** page or the **Preview** page!

TIP #60

Get Back to the Sound Page

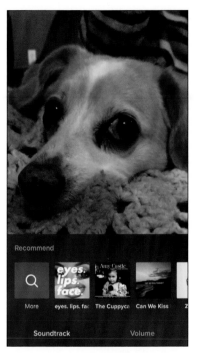

1. For the full list of **Sounds** to choose from, tap on the magnifying glass. This takes you back to where you can choose from your favorites or where you can discover new sounds.

2. For maximum views, tap **Trending** to go to a list of the most popular songs and sounds being used right now.

TIP #61

How to Go Back to Your Original Sound

Adding a **Sound** in the **Preview** page deletes your original **Sound**. If you wish to go back to that original **Sound**, don't hit the **Next** button. You'll have to hit the **return to previous button** arrow. At that point, you'll lose all your other edits as well. This goes for anything you do on the **Preview** page!

TIP #62

Adding Effects, Visuals, and More

1. Tap **Effects** for a list of visual effects, fun effects, transitions, splits, and more.

2. When you find an effect you wish to use, long press it.

3. The video will play, and in the **Preview** pane you can see the effect.

4. Release the button when you wish the effect to end.

5. Tap the return arrow if you want to try again.

6. When you're happy with the effect, make sure to tap **Save**.

7. Please note that if you use an **Effect**, you will lose any previous **Visual** you've set. And vice versa.

TIP #63

For Transitions

1. Tap **Effects** and then **Transition**.

2. Move the white bar over the small preview of the movie to where you want the transition. Or, as the thumbnail preview of your video plays, you can tap on the white bar to pause the video. Then, tap on the transition you want, and it will appear.

3. You can choose several transitions if you wish, but don't overuse them as they can get annoying!

4. You will not lose your previous effects by using transitions!

TIP #64

Manual Transitions

In video editing, a transition is what happens between two clips in order to join the clips together. Transitions can be an instant scene or change, a fade to black, a dissolving scene, a pan from one area to another, and more. In TikTok, transitions can be a lot of fun, and the best way to get good at using transitions in your videos is to practice, practice, practice . . . and watch what other creators are doing. Transitions are also useful for making your video more interesting.

TIP #65

Creating Your Own Transitions

There are dozens of user-created transitions you can learn by looking them up on YouTube. Most of these transitions are filmed in 2x time.

Some of the most popular ones are:

The Swipe: This transition gives the illusion that you have been magically transported somewhere else.

1. Hold your phone out in front of you. Make sure your phone is recording using the selfie camera. Press and hold **Record** and move the phone to the right until you are no longer in the screen. Stop recording.

2. Move to a different location. Place the phone all the way to your left (the opposite side of where you ended up in the first clip).

3. Press and hold **Record,** and bring the phone back in front of you.

The Hand Swipe: This one works similarly to the Swipe.

1. Hold your phone out in front of you. Press and hold **Record.** Move your free hand in front of the camera, obscuring yourself. Stop recording.

2. Move to a different location. Place your free hand over the camera, then press and hold **Record.** Remove your hand to reveal your new location.

Stop Motion: This mimics stop-motion movies.

1. Say you're going to unclench your fist. Slightly move your fingers away from your palm. Press and hold **Record** for just a moment. Stop recording.

2. Move your fingers a little further away from your palm. Press and hold **Record** for just a moment. Stop recording.

3. And so on until your fist is fully open.

Other transitions to learn include **The Spin** (or **Around your head**), **The Shake**, and more. We could write a whole book on transitions, but then we wouldn't get paid for this one.

TIP #66

For Split
This effect provides multiples of the video on the screen.

1. Tap **Effects** and then **Split.** Hold the **Split** you wish to apply as the video preview plays.

2. Let go when you want the split to end.

3. You will not lose previous effects when adding splits.

TIP #67

For Time
From here you can set parts of your video to go in **Reverse**, **Repeat**, or **Slow-mo**.

TIP #68

Adding Text

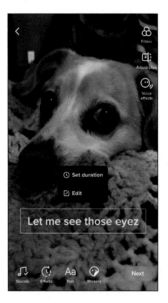

Text provides context for a lot of videos. Text can create suspense, such as, "Wait till the end!" for instance.

1. Tap the **Text** icon from the **Preview** page.

2. Use the keyboard to type your text.

3. Choose the color of the text by tapping on one of the colored circles.

4. Choose the typeface you want to use by tapping one of the typeface names. You can choose from **Classic**, **Typewriter**, **Neon**, and others.

5. Align the text to the left, right, or in the center by tapping on the centered lines icon.

6. Tap the **A** in the box to select what sort of box you want for the text.

7. Tap **Done**.

8. Now you can hold your finger to the type and move it wherever you want.

9. TikTok will let you know if your text will be interfered with by the Home screen icons or any hashtags you add.

TIP #69

Set the Duration of the Text

1. After step 7 above, Tap and release on the type to set the duration. Move the duration bars to where in the video you want the text to appear. If the whole video thumbnail is red, your text will appear for the whole shot.

2. Tap the check mark once you're happy with the placement.

3. You can keep editing the text and its placement and duration by tapping on the text.

TIP #70

Appearing and Disappearing Text

I. If you have more than one thing to say, and you want text to appear and disappear in different parts of your video, set up your first message using the instructions above.

2. Once the first text message is in place for the correct duration, tap on **Text** and set your second message. Use the same directions to set duration.

TIP #71

Angle Your Text

Want your text at an angle?

I. Place one finger at the beginning of your text block and another at the end.

2. Move your fingers until you have your text just right.

TIP #72

Change Text Size

Want your text bigger . . . or smaller?

I. Place one finger at the beginning of your text block and another at the end.

2. Move your fingers away from each other to make the text bigger.

3. Pinch fingers together to make the text smaller.

4. Play around until you have your text just the way you like it.

TIP #73

Adding Stickers from the Preview Page

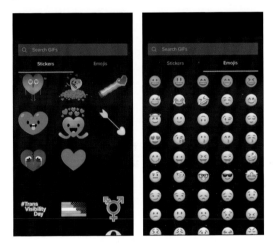

I. Tap the **Stickers** icon from the **Preview** Page.

2. From this screen you can search for stickers or emojis to add to your video.

3. Choose your sticker or emoji by tapping on it.

4. You will end up back in the preview screen where you can long press the sticker or emoji and move it around the screen until you're happy with placement.

5. Single tap on the sticker or emoji to set its duration.

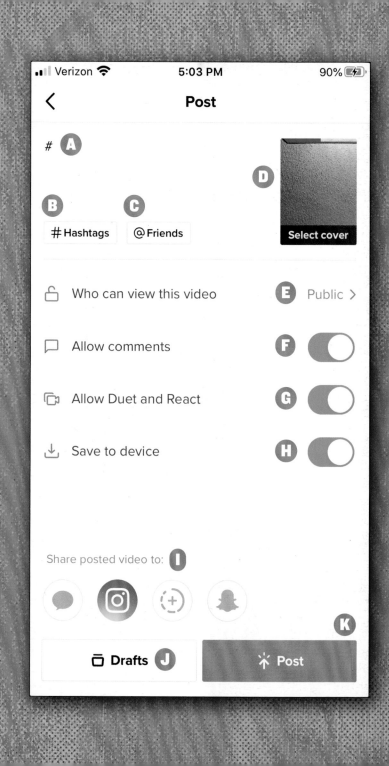

THE POST PAGE

Tap the Next button at the bottom right of the Preview page. This takes you to the third of three screens: the Post page.

A. Where you describe your video. Keep it short so you have room for hashtags!

B. Tap to add your hashtags.

C. Tag your friends on TikTok.

D. Add a cover for your video from a still.

E. Decide who can view your video.

F. Decide whether or not to allow comments.

G. Decide whether or not to allow Duets and Reactions

H. Decide whether or not you want to save your video to your phone.

I. You can decide to share your video on other social media apps.

J. If you're not ready to post, save the video to Drafts.

K. Post and wait for your followers to find you!

TIP #74

Describe Your Video

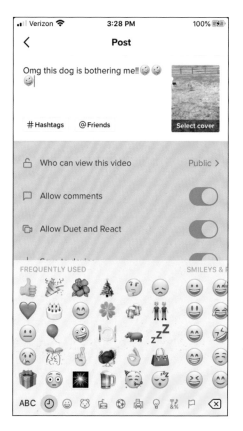

This description appears below your handle on the video.

1. Keep it short and sweet here.

2. You can also add emojis from your keyboard.

3. You can ask a question such as, "How do I look in this?" or say something that grabs your viewers' attention like, "You won't believe what happened when I tried to film this!"

TIP #75

Tag Hashtags in Your TikTok Video

1. Tap the **Hashtag** button to add tags.

2. As you type, trending hashtags will come up to help you decide what to use.

3. See pages 139–142 for more on using hashtags.

4. Remember, too many hashtags may hinder viewing the video.

TIP #76

Tag Users in Your TikTok Video

You can tag users in your TikTok video's description on the **Post** screen.

1. Tap the **@friends** button to find friends to tag. They will get a notification and perhaps will be that much more likely to view your video!

TIP #77

Change the Privacy of Your TikTok Video

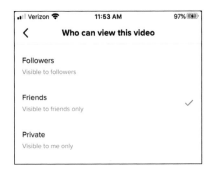

You can change the privacy of your TikTok video on the **Post** page. Tap **Who can view this video** and select one of the following options:

Public: Visible to everyone

Friends: Visible to friends only

Private: Visible to you only

You can also change your settings for all videos. Here's how:

1. Go to your **Profile** page.

2. Tap the **More** (. . .) icon in the upper right-hand corner.

3. Tap **Privacy and safety**.

4. Under **Safety**, you'll find controls for who can send you direct messages or who you can **Duet**, or who can **React**, view your liked videos, and comment on your videos.

5. If you want to filter comments, you can tap on **Comment Filters**. From there, you can filter spam and offensive comments as well as filter keywords.

TIP #78

Turn Comments Off

I. Tap the button next to **Allow comments** to turn this feature off or on. Viewers will be able to watch your video but won't be able to add any comments if you turn the feature off.

2. You can also disable **direct messages** and/or **comments** for all your TikTok videos from your **Privacy and safety** page.

TIP #79

Turn Duet/React off on your TikTok

You can disable **Duet/React.** This stops others from duetting and reacting to it. Tap the button next to **Allow Duet** and **React** to turn this feature off or on. You can also disable duets and/or reactions for all your TikTok videos from your **Privacy and safety** page.

TIP #80

Turn off Download for all TikTok Videos

If you don't want anyone downloading your video, you can disable that function.

I. Tap the button to the right of **Save.**

2. You can also disable **Downloads** for all your TikTok videos from your **Privacy and safety** page.

TIP #81

Not Quite Ready to Post?

Save your video to **Drafts** to work on it later.

I. You can find your **Drafts** on your **Profile** page. You can also save the video as a draft if you're not ready for the world to witness your brilliance quite yet. From here, you can also tag your friends so they know you're posting new content. Finally, you can share posted videos to other platforms by tapping on one of the circles at the bottom of the page.

Ready?

Tap **Post!**

I. From here, you can also choose other functions such as **Create a Live Photo from a TikTok Video** (see Tip #24 on page 48) and **Create a GIF from a TikTok video** (see Tip #25 on page 48).

TIP #82

Change Settings for Posted Videos

You can also change settings for individual videos.

I. Open the video you want to change the settings for.

2. Tap the **More** (. . .) icon. The More screen pops up at the bottom. From here you can save the video, **Duet**, **React**, Add to your favorites, and more. The icon we're interested in is **Privacy** settings. Tap it.

3. From here you can decide who can view this video:

Followers

Friends

Private (only you can see it)

4. You can also disable comments, **Duets**, and **Reacts** from this screen.

What's Next?

If you want more tips on making really good movies, head over to Chapter 5, where some simple and advanced techniques will be presented for making your movies better for the purposes of going viral.

CHAPTER 4
INTERACTING

The "social" in "social media" is an especially important reason TikTok is so popular. Yes, this app is about making memorable videos, but the reason it's so huge is that the social aspect is so central to what makes TikTok fun. We watch each other's videos, we comment on them, we tag friends, we **React** and **Duet**, we imitate and pay homage to, and come together with our shared interests. All of this boosts your profile on the app while boosting the other creators as well.

This chapter shows you how to interact with others, gives you the TikTok basics for communicating with other creators, and then delves into some tips for how to stand out and be a popular member of this community.

START WITH WHO YOU KNOW

Joining TikTok for the first time is a little bit like walking alone into a gigantic party. What's the first thing you do in that situation? Look for your friends! TikTok provides lots of ways to find people you know who are already on TikTok as well as a few ways to invite your friends to join.

TIP #83

Stay Positive
Engaging with others is fun and can lead to more people viewing your videos; however, your comments should be interesting, but positive. Don't come across as close-minded, don't harp on people's looks, and be funny but not demeaning.

TIP #84

Invite Friends to TikTok

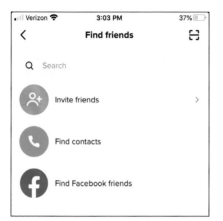

1. Got to your **Profile** page.

2. Tap the **add person** icon in the top left-hand corner.

3. Tap **Invite Friends**.

4. At this point, TikTok will need permission to access your contacts on your phone.

5. Find people you would like to invite and tap the red **Invite** button. This opens up your text messaging and prepares a text for you to send. Hit **Send** and you're good to go.

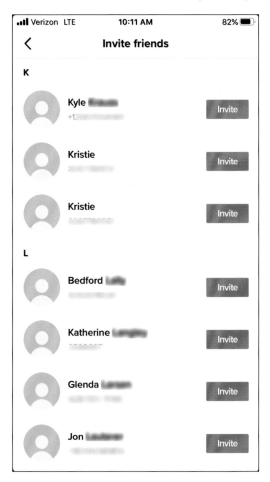

6. You can also invite friends to TikTok by tapping on the circle icons at the top of this screen. This lets you invite via Facebook, Facebook Messenger, Twitter, WhatsApp, email, and more.

TIP #85

Find Contacts

1. Once you give TikTok access to your contacts, it connects the dots, and when you tap **Find contacts**, it will list people you know who are on TikTok.

2. Click the red **Follow** button to follow their accounts. Or, if you're not sure you know them, tap on their information to go to their page.

3. As you scroll through the contacts, you'll soon run out of **Follow** options and the people on the rest of the list are not on TikTok. You can invite them to join by tapping the red **Invite** button.

TIP #86

Find Friends on Facebook

1. Tap **Find Facebook friends.**

2. Allow TikTok access by following the prompts.

3. Tap the red **Follow** button for people on Facebook you want to follow.

4. If you tap **Invite your friends to TikTok,** you will be taken to Facebook Messenger, where you can send a short message inviting Facebook friends to join.

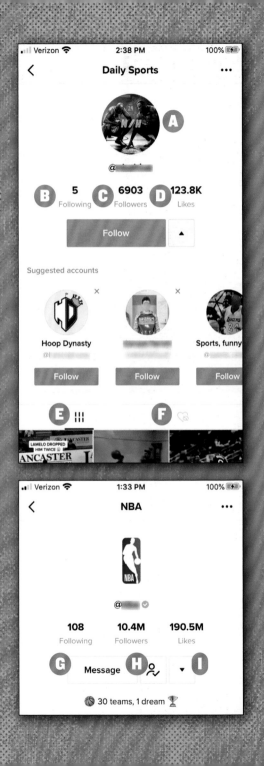

OTHER USERS' PROFILE PAGES

When you find a creator you especially like, spend some time researching and following the creators they like and who like them. This is an especially good thing to do if the creator makes videos along the lines of the kind you're trying to make. Not only will you start getting ideas from these creators, but you'll also be growing a potential list of users who will follow you one day. There are several things you can do from someone's **Profile** page.

A. Tap on their profile image to enlarge it.

B. Tap **Following** to see who the account is following.

C. Tap **Followers** to see who is following the account. You can tap on them to get to their Profile page or tap **Follow** to follow them as well.

D. Likes is the total number of likes that creator has received across all videos.

E. Tapping the two rows of vertical lines takes you to that user's videos.

F. Unless the creator has disabled it, you can press the heart to see what videos they have liked.

G. Tap **Message** to send a direct message.

H. Tapping here will unfollow the account.

I. Tap this arrow for a list of suggested accounts based on the fact you followed this one.

TIP #87

Follow Creators That Catch Your Attention

Watch a bunch of videos and start following creators who have similar interests as you, are genuinely funny, or otherwise catch your attention.

1. To follow someone from a video you're watching, long press the + sign below their profile photo in the circle on the right side of the page.

2. To follow from someone's **Profile** page, tap the photo (to the right of the video you're watching) or their handle (on the lower left side of the screen). This takes you to the creator's **Profile** page. Here you can view other videos they have made, see how many followers they have, and more.

TIP #88

Search and Find a TikTok User

The first way to find someone is from a TikTok video you're currently watching.

1. Every video shows you the creator on the right. It's the first icon, their profile photo.

2. Tap their profile picture on the right side of the page to view their profile.

3. Alternatively, when you're watching one of their videos, tap their TikTok handle in the corner.

4. Another way is from the **Discover** page. Go to **Discover** from the menu bar. From the top, search for a user.

TIP #89

Shout Outs

You can further interact with your fans by sharing their videos and even mentioning them in your videos. This can help foster loyalty and word-of-mouth recommendations.

TIP #90

View Comments . . . and Leave One

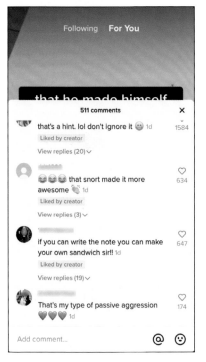

The best way to engage with other creators is to leave comments on their videos. (Remember, keep the comments interesting and positive!)

1. Once you find a video you like, tap the **Comment** icon on the right side of the screen.

2. This will take you to the video's comment screen. At the top will be the existing comments. At the bottom is space for you to add a comment.

3. Tap the @ icon to tag a user.

4. Tap the **emoji** icon to add an emoji to your comment.

5. From this screen you can also like other comments by tapping on the heart icons. This shows you're engaging with not only the user, but his or her followers as well.

6. If you want to comment on a comment, tap on the original comment. From there you will be prompted to reply.

7. If you're watching a video from, say, a user's liked videos tab, you may see the option to add comments at the bottom of the video. Tap the field, and a keyboard will pop up so you can add your comment. Then follow steps 4 and 5 above.

8. You also have the ability to **delete any comment** posted on your videos— just long press the comment, and then choose "delete."

TIP #91

Like or Dislike a TikTok Video

1. Tap the Heart icon on the right of the screen to like a video.

2. If you decide not to like the video after all, just tap the heart icon again.

DUET A TIKTOK VIDEO

The **Duet** recording feature is a great way to interact with popular TikTok creators. When you do a duet, you're recording yourself split-screen style with another video. It can be a previous video of yours or someone else's (if they haven't disabled that function). Duets can be spoofs, remixes, reactions, and actual collaborations. Artists like Lizzo, Camila Cabello, and Tove Lo have used the format to promote singles and connect with fans.

1. Tap the **Share** icon on the right side of the video. If you don't see the **Share** icon, that creator doesn't allow sharing or reacting.

2. Tap **Duet**. This takes you to a modified **Camera** page with the original video on the right. The video you're about to shoot is on the left. From here you can also add effects, etc.

3. When done recording, you can further edit from the **Preview** screen.

4. Tap the **Next** button. From the **Post** screen you can adjust your preferences.

5. Tap **Post** to publish your **Duet**.

TIP #92

Duet a Duet

Yes, you can duet with an existing duet video. It gets messy, but it's also fun.

TIP #93

Ask for It

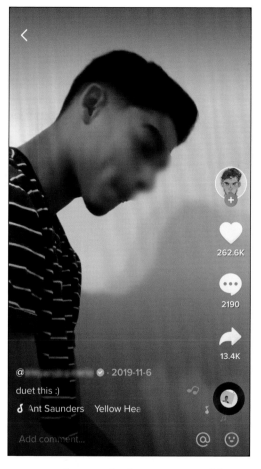

You can create videos with the purpose of having others **Duet** with it. These can be funny monologues for others to respond to, funny reactions, and more. You can request duets in the description.

REACT TO A VIDEO

Here, you're reacting to a video that shows up picture-in-picture style. The original video shows up as a small screen that you can move to where you want it.

1. Tap the **Share** icon on the right side of the video. If you don't see the **Share** icon, that user doesn't allow sharing or reacting.

2. Tap **React**. This takes you to a modified **Camera** page with the original video in the left hand corner. From here you can also add effects, etc.

3. When done recording, you can further edit from the **Preview** page. You can also position where you want your overlay video to play alongside the original.

4. Tap the **Next** button. From the **Post** page you can adjust your preferences.

5. Tap **Post** to publish your reaction.

TIP #94

Fun React Video

Find a video of someone asking questions. Respond to the questions in your React video. Be creative and silly!

TIP #95

Duet and Reaction Safety

You have full control over whether or not others can perform duets or react to your videos. As with any social media platform, things can turn mean quickly. If you're inviting mockery, that's fine, but if you're not, you can manage the settings for your profile as well as for each of your videos. To adjust your settings, go to the **Profile** page.

I. Tap the **More** (...) icon at the top right-hand corner of the screen.

2. Tap **Privacy and safety**.

3. Under **Safety**, tap **Who can Duet** with your videos or **Who can React** to your videos.

4. You have three choices:
- **Everyone:** all members of the TikTok community.
- **Friends:** only your TikTok friends.
- **No one:** This disables the **Duet** function for all members.

5. This change takes effect for all future videos you shoot.

6. See Tip #79 on page 95 for adjusting **Duet** and **React** settings for individual videos.

USING YOUR INBOX

The inbox is where you can view all the activity your account is generating, such as likes, comments, mentions, and more.

1. Tap on the **Inbox** at the bottom of the Home screen.

2. From here you can view all activity, or tap the top middle of the screen to choose what to view. You can see your **Likes**, **Comments**, **Mentions**, and when someone new follows you.

3. **From TikTok** shows you messages from them.

TIP #96

Send Direct Messages

You can send direct messages to users you are following or who are following you.

1. Tap on the **Inbox** at the bottom of the **Home** page.

2. Tap on the paper airplane icon at the top right-hand corner of the page.

3. Tap the plus icon at the top right-hand corner of the page.

4. Choose who you want to send a direct message to, then compose your message. Tap **Send** when ready.

TIP #97

View Direct Messages

1. Tap on the Inbox at the bottom of the **Home** page.

2. Tap the **envelope** at the top corner of your page.

TIP #98

Find Out Who Viewed Your Profile Screen

1. Tap the **Inbox** icon.

2. Read any notifications that are in there.

3. If you see one that says, "[insert username] and many others checked your profile yesterday," tap on it. This will then show you all the users who visited your profile in the last 24 hours. This updates just about every 24 hours, so check in regularly.

TIP #99

Do You Need to Go Pro?

The main reason for switching to a pro account is to view statistics of your posts. You can get insights on a video's performance for the last week or month. You can get information on the gender of your viewers, which countries they come from, and more. It might be more information than you need, but if you're an avid creator, check it out. It's free and you can always cancel it if you don't want it anymore. If you spend $1,000 or more a year on TikTok or maintain a $2,500 balance, your account automatically goes Pro.

TIP #100

Switch to a Pro Account

1. Go to your **Profile** page, and tap the **More** (. . .) icon.

2. Tap **Manage My account**.

3. Tap **Switch to Pro Account**. Your account will be switched to **Public** once you go to a pro account, which means all of your posts will be public.

4. There will be a new **Analytics** option that you can view from **Settings**. Tap it to see your charts.

TIKCODES

Another way to find and get in touch with other users is through TikCodes. Every user is assigned a TikCode that others can scan to quickly get to your profile. One of the best ways to use your own TikCode is to post it to your other social media platforms, such as Instagram or Facebook. If someone likes your content there, they can easily get to your TikTok page by scanning the TikCode. To find your TikCode:

1. Go to the Home page and tap the **Me** icon to get to your Profile page.

2. Tap the **More** (. . .) icon at the top right-hand corner of the screen.

3. Under **Account**, tap **TikCode**. Your TikCode will appear with an option to save it to your phone.

4. You can also find your TikCode from the **Discover** page. Tap **Discover** from the **Home** page, tap the **Scan** button at the top right-hand corner of the page, and then tap **MyTikCode** at the bottom of this page.

TIP #101

Scan Someone Else's TikCode

1. Tap the **Me** icon to get to your **Profile** page.

2. Tap the **More** (. . .) icon at the top right-hand corner of the screen.

3. Under **Account**, tap **TikCode**. Tap the **Scan** icon at the bottom of the screen.

4. Align the code to the square in the middle of the screen. The code will automatically register and you'll be taken to that user's profile page.

5. You can also access this function from the **Discover** screen. Tap **Discover** from the **Home** page and then tap the **Scan** button at the top right-hand corner of the screen.

CURATE YOUR FOLLOWERS

TikTok gives you the ability to control who sees your videos (to an extent) as well as how broadly you want your videos to be sent out. Here's a rundown of the tools and settings you can use as you become a part of this community.

Private Vs. Public Accounts

As TikTok says, "Whether you want to share your videos with the world or just your closest friends, the choice is up to you."

By default, your account is public. That means any TikTok user can view your videos, post comments, film a duet or reaction, and more. But it's easy to change this in your

Privacy Settings. With a private account, you can approve or deny follower requests. Only users you've approved can follow you and view your videos and likes.

Note: Your existing followers won't disappear if you turn your account private.

TIP #102

How to Remove a Follower

If you no longer want someone to follow your account, you can remove them from your Followers page or their profile. When a user is removed from your followers, your videos will not appear in their **Following** feed.

1. Tap the **More** icon (. . .) next to their username and tap **Remove** this follower.

2. To remove a follower from their **Profile** page, tap the **More** icon (. . .) in the top right hand corner and tap **Remove** this follower.

Note: If you have a public account, they will still have the opportunity to re-follow your account. If you have a private account, they will need to send another follow request before they are allowed to follow you again.

TIP #103

How to Block a User

TikTok allows you to block users. TikTok says, "We encourage users to follow the community guidelines and treat their fellow TikTok users with respect. If someone violates these rules by bullying or harassing you, you can block that user in addition to removing them from your followers. When you block a user they will not be able to contact you, view, or interact with any of your content."

1. Go to the user's **Profile** page.

2. Tap the **More** icon (. . .).

3. Tap **Block**, and then confirm.

TIP #104

How to Report a User

You can report a user for breaking the rules or doing something inappropriate such as imitating you or a celebrity, posting inappropriate content, or posting misleading information. See Chapter 6 for more on this.

1. Go to the user's **Profile** page.

2. Tap the **More** icon (. . .) in the upper right-hand corner of the screen.

3. Tap **Report**. From here, there are several dropdown menus where you can choose the activity you wish to report. For instance, **Posting Inappropriate Content** opens up to a list of behaviors such as Dangerous organizations and individuals, Animal cruelty, Suicide or self-harm, Harassment or bullying, and more.

Understand Your Following

Pay attention to who is following you and what they are saying. Pay attention to the comments and who is making them. Follow them back if you like what they're saying. Give them a shout-out by name. If you get enough followers, you can figure out what age range is most interested in your content as well as what is working and what's not by the number of likes you get. If you find a particular type of video keeps getting more likes than other types, stick to what is working the best.

Reply to All Comments

Every time you respond to a comment you receive, you instill a feeling of goodwill among your viewers that may be rewarded with more views, likes, and comments.

Ask Your Viewers for Feedback

Ask them to propose new ideas, subjects for you to cover, clothes to wear, or new locations. The more you engage, the more invested everyone will feel in your brand and personality.

Not Working Out?

If your videos get 100 or fewer views, you're going to end up with a zombie account. Delete the account and start over again after a while.

TIP #105

Want More Than One Account?

It's not that easy to get views and followers on TikTok. Some try to enhance their chances by creating more than one account. At this point, TikTok allows users to add four additional accounts for a total of five. Here's what you do . . . but read the note below before committing to this:

1. Make sure you have the latest version of the app.

2. From the **Home** page, tap the **Me** icon in the lower right-hand corner of the screen.

3. Tap the account name in the top center of your **Profile** page.

4. Tap **Add account**.

5. You will go through the same process you did in Chapter 1; however, you must sign up with a different email or phone number. For instance, if you used a phone number to sign up for your first account, use your email for the second account.

Signing up for multiple accounts on one phone flags you as a business account. That means you will be de-prioritized unless you're a paying advertiser! If you still want more than one profile, use multiple devices and keep separate accounts on each one.

VERIFIED ACCOUNTS

Every now and then you may see a blue checkmark next to someone's handle. It could be a famous musician, an influencer, or a brand. That means they've been verified by TikTok and TikTok has confirmed that the account actually belongs to the user it represents. This system is in place to help users make better decisions about who they are following . . . building trust among the highest profile users. A checkmark means you are following the real deal and not an imposter.

TIP #106

Don't Be Fooled by Fake Checks

A blue checkmark in a bio or anywhere else besides next to a user's handle is fake.

TIP #107

Tips for Getting Verified

You can't ask TikTok to get verified. But you should do everything in your power to get TikTok's attention so you will get verified. First off, you need at least 1,000 followers. Here are some of the other factors TikTok looks for when considering verified badges:

- Are you popular—like, really popular?
- Do you provide a constant stream of quality content?
- Are you already someone who is famous?
- Is the account authentic, unique, and active?
- Does it adhere to TikTok's Community Guidelines and Terms of Service?
- Are you working toward gaining more followers?

CHAPTER 5
GOING VIRAL

here is no exact science to going viral on TikTok, but there are steps to take to make it more likely that you'll be the next big thing. Sure, there are some TikTok creators who post a couple of videos and go viral instantly. The reality for every else, however, is that there are millions of videos on TikTok, so going viral is a combination of skill, luck, and intentionality. So, if you're in it to win it, it pays to pay attention to what you're doing. This includes doing your research, fine-tuning your account, mastering the **For You** page, and creating videos that grab people's attention. This chapter delves into all the tools available on TikTok and how to use them to get more followers, likes, and comments, and how to (hopefully) hit it big.

DOING YOUR RESEARCH

As spontaneous as TikTok looks, the most successful users study trends, users, video techniques, and more.

TIP #108

Follow the Latest Trends on the Discover Screen

This page shows you the most popular trends on the app right now.

1. From the **Home** page, tap the **Discover** icon at the bottom of the screen.

2. Type in words or phrases in the **Search** area. From here you can find users, videos, sounds, and hashtags.

3. Scroll through the trending hashtags.

TIP #109

Know Your Influencers

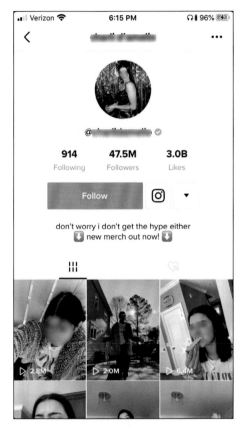

Influencers are the heart of TikTok. They have millions of followers and up to a billion or more likes across all their videos. They appear on late-night talk shows, at the NBA All-Star game, and more. Research the influencers and follow them first. Get to know what they do and what makes them so popular. This is also a good way to get ahead of a trend or a new challenge.

As of right now, here are a list of some of today's top TikTok influencers:

Rank	Username	Owner	Followers (millions)	Likes (millions)	Description
1	@charlidamelio	Charli D'Amelio	46.0	2895.9	Dancer and Social Media Personality
2	@lorengray	Loren Gray	42.0	2307.1	Singer and Social Media Personality
3	@zachking	Zach King	39.7	404.4	Filmmaker and Social Media Personality
4	@tiktok	TikTok	38.3	211.9	Social Media Platform
5	@riyaz.14	Riyaz Aly	34.4	1493.8	Social Media Personality
6	@babyariel	Baby Ariel	31.9	1729.1	Singer, Actress, and Social Media Personality
7	@addisonre	Addison Rae	31.3	1395.6	Dancer and Social Media Personality
8	@spencerx	Spencer Polanco White	27.2	592.5	Beatboxer and Social Media Personality
9	@mr_faisu_07	Faisal Shaikh	26.6	1552.8	Social Media Personality
10	@gilmhercroes	Gilmher Croes	25.6	656.9	Social Media Personality

TIP #110

Reach Out to the Big Wigs

Getting an endorsement from or a collaboration with a popular TikTok user is a quick way to get likes and followers. However, it's difficult to reach out to TikTok users. You can't direct message anyone unless you follow them and they follow you back. So, if you want to reach out to an influencer on TikTok, the easiest way might be via their other social media platforms, such as Instagram, Twitter, Facebook, or YouTube.

TIP #111

The Follow/Unfollow Influencers Trick

This is a neat trick that may help you get the attention of an influencer.

1. Follow an influential user in your niche. Interact with their videos and comment on them. Try your best to get upvoted.

2. Then, unfollow the influencer. Repeat several times. Why? When you refollow someone, you appear higher on their Followers screen, increasing the likelihood of users viewing your profile.

TIP #112

What You'll Learn from Watching Countless TikTok Videos

Getting famous is about being original . . . but not too original! It's more about bringing your own creative and innovative style to what's already being done. Or, to put it more simply: Put a twist on something that's already out there and popular. The trick is to catch a trend on its way up! Being cringeworthy can work! Cringe videos on TikTok used to be a big part of what was out there.

Being relatable counts. It's not the users who obviously want to be big that go viral, but rather, the users who are able to create a personality or a character that people relate to.

Influencers start a community that supports them. The influencer's content at that point is about adding more information to that character.

The one thing you'll notice about some of the most liked videos is that it sure looks like everyone is having a ton of fun. If you're shooting videos and not really enjoying yourself, it will probably be apparent.

The most popular users know how to tell a story . . . even the dancers. For instance, the dancers change locations, clothing, and music, and they're always playing with effects. If you can create a narrative, your audience will be excited about what's next.

Outright copycats and users who post videos available elsewhere, don't usually gain much traction.

TIP #113

Check Out the Sounds

Music is such an integral part of the TikTok experience. Jumping on a "sound" bandwagon at the right time can get you a lot of likes.

As you're watching videos, tap on the sound icon at the right-hand bottom of the screen. There you will see the name of the song as well as the cover of the song that you can tap on to hear.

You can add the song to your favorites to use later on. Under the artist is the number of videos that have used that sound. Obviously the higher the number, the bigger its impact on the TikTok community.

TIP #114

Know Your Niche

You can't really fine-tune anything until you know what you're all about. The very best TikTok users know their lane and pretty much stay in it. It's a little bit easier to find and understand your niche if you are a dancer, musician, tracer, cheerleader, or other athlete, chef, comedian, singer, actor, or gamer. But even if you're just a meme-obsessed user who likes to post fun videos, you can find your "people." Start on the **Discovery** page and type in words and phrases that have to do with your niche. See what pops up and get inspiration. Take notes and then as you start posting content, reach out to your niche peers. Follow them, like their content, and post on their videos. Once they follow you back, you can direct message them for possible collaborations.

FINE-TUNING YOUR ACCOUNT

Perhaps you blindly set up your TikTok account with no aspirations other than taking videos of your cats, but now you know you want to go viral. What to do? Your first steps should be to fine-tune your account.

TIP #115

Create a Strong and Catchy TikTok Username

Your username on any social media platform is your brand. And that's especially true of TikTok. If you have a username on other platforms, use it in order to be consistent. No reason to confuse your followers. If you're new to the game, however, here are some things to take into account:

What is your brand "persona" going to be? For instance, if you want to post cooking videos, you might want to use food-related words in your username. This makes it easier for users to find you.

Use your own name or some form of it. If your name is already taken, use special characters until you have a username no one else has. One of the reasons for using your own name is that followers may feel closer to you. Many of the most followed TikTok influencers simply use their names.

Make sure your username isn't offensive in your native language . . . or anyone else's! Google your chosen name and see what comes up.

TIP #116

Need Help with a Username?

If you're having trouble coming up with a creative username try one of the many username generators on the web. We like spinxo.com because we knew we wanted the word "rooster" in the name, but we weren't sure what else.

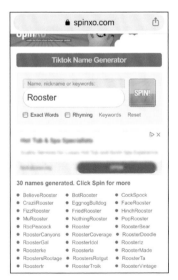

Go to spinxo.com and type in your name. It will generate 30 names. If you don't like any of them, tap **Spin** for a new selection.

Spinxo also has a function that lets you check username availability on different social networks. Other generators also have this function.

TIP #117

How to Change Your TikTok Username

Once you have an account, tap the Me icon in the lower right-hand corner. Tap **Edit profile**. Tap on **Username** to edit it. Type in your new username. **Save**. If the name is already taken, you will receive a notice, and you'll have to try something else. Remember, there are millions of TikTok users out there, so you may have to get creative!

TIP #118

Up Your Bio Quote Game

If you're looking to attract more people to your profile, consider writing something really clever or funny or inspirational for your bio quote. Keep your target audience in mind, and don't be afraid to let your bio reflect your profession or talent you're showcasing in your videos.

TIP #119

Sampling of Cool Bios

- If it's all about going viral: Might as well follow me now before I get famous.
- If you don't want to get specific but have a vibe in mind: Live, love, TikTok.
- If you love baseball: Dope clips and bat flips.
- If you want to showcase where you live: 22 California welcome to the show.
- If you want to get ahead of the curve: I probably don't like you either.
- If you want to be clever: You look lost . . . follow me.
- If you want more followers: Name reveal at 20k!

TIP #120

Link to your Instagram or YouTube Account

This helps you create crossover interest and makes sure your followers can reach your content on all platforms.

1. On your **Profile** page, tap the **Edit profile** button.

2. Tap **Instagram** or **YouTube**. This takes you to the login page of these apps. Log in and follow the instructions.

3. Once you're done, an icon appears next to the **Follow** button on your **Profile** page.

4. You can also give followers your handles in your bio or use them as your username.

MASTERING THE "FOR YOU" SCREEN

TikTok uses algorithms to determine which videos show up on the **For You** screen, which is where TikTok features popular and trending videos. (But, interestingly, the algorithm is just as likely to highlight anonymous creators with few or even 0 likes!) It's just about everyone's goal to get their videos on this page, and there's no real way to gain a foothold in this community without getting and staying on the **For You** screen. But there are tried-and-true things you can do to help, and most of it involves using the very tools TikTok gives you to create your content.

Note: Figuring out how to beat TikTok's algorithm has been a fun, albeit frustrating pastime for many TikTok users. We have all attempted to figure out how to beat the system, but few have succeeded! The best way to "beat" the algorithm is to be funnier, better, and cooler than everyone else. If that hasn't worked—and believe us, some of the coolest and funniest users haven't cracked the code yet—don't get overwhelmed by all the superstitious stuff online or the conspiracy theories. Spend your time instead on your content.

TIP #121

Post . . . Often!

The biggest tool in your toolbox is your content. TikTok has handed you an extremely powerful tool for creating amazing videos. But how often should you post? People who study TikTok say that it pays to be hyperactive on the app. Others say you can't post enough. Keep 'em coming, and combined with lots of commenting and liking, you will be rewarded with a video on the **For You** page! The most popular users post anywhere from two to seven (and more) times a day! That's commitment for you. So, if you're worried about the balance between quality vs. quantity, lean a little toward quantity, especially when you're first starting out.

TIP #122

Research Hashtags

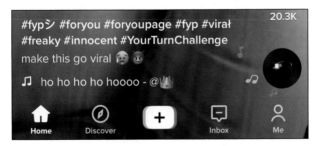

TikTok runs on hashtags! Knowing which hashtags are trending is an important way to get noticed and blow up your following. Discover the trending hashtags from the **Discover** icon on your home screen. From there, you'll see the top trends. If you shoot a video that follows the trend, don't forget to add the hashtag that corresponds to it. That way, when someone searches the hashtag, your video gets included in the results. Remember, you don't have to be original—just do something that's already there with your own special twist.

TIP #123

Know Your Calendar

When planning what to shoot for the upcoming month, note any holidays and decide what you want to do to celebrate. And then, when the hashtags for that holiday start showing up, you're ahead of the game with content ready to post with the hashtag. For instance, check out #thanksgiving. It blew up in 2019. Even if you're not sure how the holiday trend will play out, you'll know something is coming.

TIP #124

Hashtags That Work (a lot of the time)

Use the hashtags #fyp, #foryourpage, or any other combination of those words. Some believe it helps their videos get on the page. Others include #trending, #tiktok, #funny, #comedy, #meme, #followforfollowback, #dance, etc.

TIP #125

What's Up with #Xyzcba

You may notice some videos with the hashtag #xyzcba. It's used a lot like #fyp to hopefully boost your video's chances

of getting you the fyp. It's based on nothing more than a rumor that spread throughout the community. But . . . since so many people have been using the hashtag, it may now be an effective way to boost viewers since it's trending. So, even though it's a rumor, it's a rumor that may have proven itself true just because so many people believed it.

TIP #126

How to Hashtag Successfully

Some ascribe to what is called the stair-stepping method of using hashtags strategically. This is how it works:

1. Start with a hashtag that has a small but decent number of views. Perhaps instead of #animals, you could get specific with #kangaroo, for instance. The thinking here is that the competition for this hashtag isn't as fierce as one that has millions and millions of videos and views. This will give you an easier shot at gaining some traction.

2. That's why, after using your more specific and less popular hashtag, you go in with the big guns: #fyp, #comedy, #tiktok, and #trending. Try it out!

TIP #127

Hashtag Success

Some users grow their followers by using the hashtags #dancewithme, #duetwithme, etc., basically inviting everyone to not only post videos of their versions of dance moves and duets, but to also tag their videos with their hashtag—providing free advertising while also creating a community.

TIP #128

Jump on the New Tools

If TikTok launches a new effect or other editing tool, jump on it. Learn how to use it and post using it as soon as possible.

TikTok will likely reward these videos with a trip to the FYP to help promote the new effect.

TIP #129

Use Trending Sounds in Your Videos

If you see that a particular sound is getting a lot of attention, quickly create your own videos with it. Popular sounds will attract more users to your videos. Even if you have to lower the volume for the songs and raise the video's original sound, as long as the song can be heard, followers will be drawn to the popular song and check it out on your video. Also, make sure the song matches the content you are creating. A disconnect will be noticed and swiped. For instance, the song "Chasing Dragons" is used primarily by recovering addicts to tell their recovery stories. If you use that song to introduce some new dance moves, you will get more than a few negative comments and lose followers.

TIP #130

How to Find Out What Songs Are Trending?

1. Once you've identified TikTok's top users, research what songs they are using. Most likely these songs will trend very quickly. Get ahead of the curve and use the same sound quickly.

2. Tap on the **Discover** icon and check out the trending hashtags. Many times these trends or challenges rely on a specific song.

Watch the videos in a trending video, and if they use the same song, use that song to add your own take on the trend.

TIP #131

Make Your Own Sounds

TikTok allows sounds to be shared from one user to the next . . . with the sound creator getting credit. That means if you have a catchy soundbite or other awesome sound that the community grabs ahold of and runs with, that will drive traffic to your page.

TIP #132

Do Challenges

Challenges can arise seemingly out of nowhere or be sponsored by an organization or company. Either way, knowing about trending challenges is a great way to get noticed and liked. Challenges are usually a combination of sound, action (or dance), and text and involve dancing, singing, or performing some sort of stunt.

TIP #133

Post at the Right Time

It's great to make it to the **For You** page, but what if no one is awake to watch it? When do other users in your niche post most often? Post around the same times. If that's difficult to figure out, set a schedule for yourself. For instance, if you're posting four videos a day, post at 9:00 a.m., 1:00 p.m., 5:00 p.m., and 9:00 p.m. Then, get some rest.

TIP #134

Cross-platform Sharing

TikTok videos end up all over the place. Users share their content on other social networks all the time. Integration for sharing on these apps and others is built in. So, don't think you're going to go viral through TikTok alone. Share to your Instagram account, Facebook page, and more.

MAKING MOVIES

You have 15 seconds to impress. Low-quality videos are going to get swiped up quicker than you can say "viral? NOT!" Here are a bunch of tips for making your movies look better.

Things to Remember When Planning Your Videos

TikTok rewards videos that get viewed to the end and re-watched. Therefore, keep your videos short and interesting. Don't film 60-second videos until you're more established . . . and only . . . and even then, post long videos sparingly; remember, long videos sparingly. Remember, we're living in a short-attention span world!

Stay in your lane. Don't get caught up in being so original that your viewers don't recognize your brand anymore. Focus instead on putting your own personal touch on what's trending. TikTok rewards users who are consistent about their content. So, if your first ten videos are all dances, keep on dancing. Same goes for if you're focusing on memes.

Don't then veer off into cheerleading videos until you're more established and can take more risks.

Since you will not be rewarded for being overly experimental (or, quite frankly, too original), once you pick your content theme and stick with it, you will gain traction within that category. If you suddenly shift gears, it will be like starting over.

Follow the latest trends, hashtags, memes, challenges, and more. The more you pay attention to these things, the better you'll get at anticipating them instead of catching them on the way down. These sorts of things peak quickly and disappear just as fast sometimes.

Don't forget that TikTok prefers portrait (vertical) videos that fill the phone's screen. Shooting your videos landscape (horizontal) doesn't look as good on the app. If it can't be helped, you can use the black bands above and below the video to place funny text.

Clean yourself up. Well-groomed users tend to do better than slobs, although sometimes this depends on your niche. Always look well rested, fresh, and really into what you are doing.

Move around a lot. Even if a video is close-up on your face, use varied facial expressions. Exaggerate your anger, sadness, joy, and other emotions. Don't underestimate your eyebrows. And if for some reason, you can't move around for a particular video, rely on varied and interesting sound effects.

TIP #135

Use Last-Second Reveals

For instance, if there's a joke or a pratfall, wait until the very end to reveal it. Also, don't promise a reveal that never arrives. Tricking someone into watching to the end will not garner much love from the community.

TIP #136

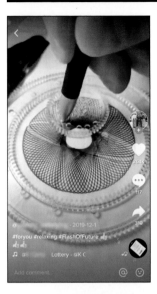

Make an Oddly Satisfying Video

These types of videos focus on actions that provide a sense of satisfaction, such as leveling an overflowing cup of flour with a credit card or organizing Legos pieces.

TIP #137

Are You an Artist?

If so, you can film your creative process. Experiment with stop-motion filming to show your drawing come together in 15 seconds . . . even if it took you hours to do.

TIP #138

Doing Stunts?

Make sure your stunt doesn't hurt anyone or scare someone to the point of making them feel overly uncomfortable. Safe stunts can trend really well on TikTok.

TIP #139

Text Dos and Don'ts

Text provides more context for your videos. It can also distract from the main event. Here are some dos and don'ts when using text:

Do

. . . provide context when needed. A guy crash-landing on his skis is cool, but knowing it's your friend is even cooler.

. . . tell viewers to "wait for it." It helps get you views . . . especially if there is something to wait for at the end of the video. If there isn't, telling viewers to "wait for it" becomes a don't!

. . . invite viewers to tag someone. For example, "Tag someone with an ugly jump shot."

. . . answer questions posed in your text in the video.

. . . introduce yourself!

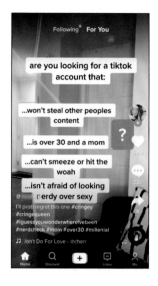

Don't

. . . call your video "The most incredible video I've ever seen," unless it truly is incredible. You can use text to get viewers to the end of your text, but if they are let down, they won't like your video or follow you.

. . . Misspell words, unless you are doing so on purpose. Telling your followers that a video "diserves" a repost makes it feel like you rushed it.

. . . don't place the text where the hashtags and handle will be.

TIP #140

Location, Location, Location

Vary your locations for your videos. If everything you share is from the same location in your bedroom, people may get bored. Also, if you are shooting in your room, clean it up! A sloppy room is distracting.

TIP #141

The Bathroom Effect

Anecdotal evidence suggests that videos shot in the bathroom outperform videos shot elsewhere. Why?

In many cases, you have great lighting. The vanity lights used each morning can be used for lighting your video. Yellow lights don't make for great lighting.

Great acoustics. All those tiles and ceramic pieces help sound carry.

The setting is intimate, but also kind of sterile and provides a "Hey, we just thought of this funny video while we were brushing our teeth," vibe as opposed to something that is painstakingly staged.

Using the mirror also gives off a vibe of something that wasn't overly planned out ahead of time . . . even if it was.

So, overall, the bathroom sneakily provides production value without your personality coming off as pretentious.

Dirty bathrooms with your stuff all over don't make very good locations. Also, if you have a bathroom with busy wallpaper, find somewhere else to shoot. Busy backgrounds aren't pleasing to look at in videos.

TIP #142

Bathroom Videos to Try

Take a shot of yourself in the bathroom mirror every day for a year. Create a video that shows how you changed.

Dance with someone else in the bathroom. Turn off the light. When the light switches back on, you're in each other's clothes.

TIP #143

Get Good Lighting

Poorly lit videos won't get liked. Lighting is such a crucial part of your production, as the better the lighting, the more it will catch and keep people's attention. Ways to avoid bad lighting?

Shoot some test videos in different places in your home at different times of day. Where is the lighting the best in the morning? The afternoon? Before dinner?

Sunny day? Take advantage of the natural light and head outside for several videos. (You don't have to post them all at once!)

Mornings are often a great time to shoot if you have enough east-facing windows.

If you want to get super serious, purchase a light ring. You'll often see light rings used by influencers and other users when they post, "how did they make that video" videos.

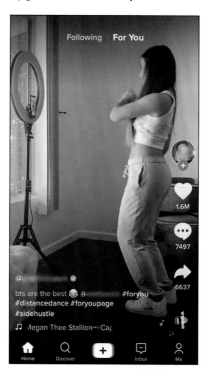

TIP #144

Buy a Tripod

Buy a tripod for your phone. Check out UBeesize Portable and Adjustable Camera Stand Holder as it's great for table-top shooting, and it comes with a remote control so you can move things around before you shoot. For outdoor shooting or when a table isn't readily available, try Ravelli's Lightweight Aluminum Phone Tripod.

TIP #145

Dancing with a Friend?

It's not always easy to film two people dancing side by side. So, have one person stand to one side and have the second person stand further back and on the other side.

TIP #146

Advanced Editing Tools

Even though you can do all your editing from the TikTok app, many top influencers shoot their videos outside of the app and use outside editing tools. Some of the most popular tools include Adobe Premier Pro, Adobe After Effects, Adobe Lightroom, and Adobe Photoshop. These are expensive tools and not necessary for most users. You can also try some of the free editors out there such as BeeCut and Quik.

TIP #147

Lock Your Focus

If you're moving around a lot in your video, the phone's camera may zoom in and out attempting to keep everything in focus. It makes your video look amateurish. To avoid this, lock your focus.

1. Launch the Camera app.

2. Long press the screen to choose the part of the image you want to focus on.

3. Don't let go until you see an AE/AF Lock banner appear at the top of the screen.

DON'T GET BANNED

There are a few ways to get banned. One way is through your content. Common sense should help, but so should TikTok's Community Guidelines. TikTok bans videos that promote: dangerous individuals and organizations, illegal activities and regulated goods, violent and graphic content, dangerous acts (suicide and self-harm), hate speech, harassment and bullying, adult nudity and sexual acts, predatory or grooming behavior toward minors, and spam.

Also, avoid the following:

- Impersonating other individuals or organizations in order to deceive the public. Parody, commentary, and fan accounts are allowed, as long as you're not misleading anyone.
- Providing misinformation that could cause harm to the community or to the public.
- Creating hoaxes.
- Publishing content that violates copyright, trademark, or other intellectual property rights.

What's Spam?

In TikTok's view, spam is content or activity that seeks to artificially inflate popularity on the platform. TikTok frowns upon posting videos about this as well as trying any of the following:

- Sharing instructions on how to artificially increase views, likes, followers, shares, or comments.
- Attempting to or engaging in selling or buying views, likes, followers, shares, or comments.
- Promoting artificial traffic generation services.
- Operating multiple accounts under false or fraudulent pretenses, including coordinated attempts to manufacture inauthentic activity, distribute commercial spam, or otherwise coordinate a scaled violation of TikTok policies.

What's a Shadow Ban?

Being shadow banned means you will not show up in the **For You** page or in search results because at least one of your videos is in violation of TikTok's Community Guidelines. You can still post videos and react on others' videos. TikTok will not let you know if you've been shadow banned. The only way to know if you're banned is to closely watch the stats of your new videos. If your numbers have dipped a lot, you've been banned. Remove the offending content, and you should be back to normal in a few days.

Beware!

There are many services out there that promise you a verification badge, more followers and likes, and more. These will not get you anywhere . . . except banned.

TIP #148

How to Keep Your Parody Account from Getting Banned

1. Your TikTok bio should indicate that your account is a fan, commentary, or parody account and that it is not affiliated with the subject of the account. The bio can include words or hashtags such as "parody," "fake," "fan," or "commentary."

2. Your nickname should indicate that your account is not affiliated or managed by the subject of the account.

3. Your username (for example, @username) should indicate that you are a fan, parody, or commentary account.

MAKING MONEY

You can make money on TikTok, but it's not as direct as what you can do with say, YouTube or other platforms. TikTok doesn't pay its top influencers and creators, nor does it offer incentives. It simply isn't built around monetization. So, while you're using your creativity to make great content, you'll need to direct some of that creativity to making money. Thankfully, lots of TikTok community members are making a pretty penny, and you can try what they've done as well. The first thing you have to do is wait. You need content, likes, and followers first.

TIP #149

Try Live Streaming

One way to earn money on TikTok is through live streaming. This is a feature that's only available to users who have more than 1,000 followers. Live streaming allows users to interact with followers and fans, answer questions, and more. During a live stream, followers can buy coins (with real money) and then tip the live streamer. The live streamer can convert the coins to diamonds, which he or she can cash out via PayPal.

TIP #150

Add Coins to Your Balance

TikTok Coins are an in-app currency that you buy with real money. You can buy Emojis and Diamonds with Coins to give to someone as appreciation for their effort. Once you have bought your TikTok Coins, they are stored in your Wallet. They are nonrefundable.

1. Go to your **Profile** page.

2. Tap the **More** [. . .] icon.

3. Select **Balance**.

4. Hit **Recharge**.

5. Select an option for the number of coins you want to buy.

6. Confirm your purchase on the next page.

TIP #151

Use TikTok to Promote Your Products

If you already have an online store or service that you provide, you can promote it on TikTok to generate traffic to your website. For example, if you're a crafter, you can provide fun, crafty ideas and then direct followers to your website that conveniently sells the supplies they need to do the crafts in your videos.

TIP #152

Get Your Followers to Follow You Everywhere

Once you've built up a following, invite them to follow you on YouTube, Instagram, Snapchat, and Twitter, where making money is a lot easier.

TIP #153

Sponsor Stuff

Brands and companies can choose to sponsor your content, and you earn money directly from the sponsors. You have to be a pretty big deal to get a sponsor's attention!

CHAPTER 6
TAKING CARE OF YOURSELF

TikTok wants people watching, sharing, liking, and making videos. But it also wants to make sure you're not avoiding other responsibilities such as eating, working, or going to school. TikTok has created Digital Wellbeing as a way to help you take care of yourself, and has added a lot of other safety measures to keep you feeling good about being part of the community.

TIP #154

Set up Screen Time Management

Want to limit your screen time while on TikTok?

1. Go to your **Profile** screen.

2. Tap the **More** (. . .) icon in the top right hand corner.

3. Tap **Digital Wellbeing**.

4. Screen Time Management is automatically set in the **Off** position. Tap **Off**. This will take you to a page where you can set a time limit for app usage for your device. After reaching the time limit, you have to enter a passcode to keep using the app.

5. Set the time limit and tap **Turn on Screen Time Management**.

TIP #155

Set Up Restricted Mode

This mode helps limit the appearance of content that may not be appropriate for some audiences.

1. Go to your **Profile** screen.

2. Tap the **More** (. . .) icon in the top right hand corner.

3. Tap **Digital Wellbeing**.

4. Tap **Off** by **Restricted Mode**.

5. Tap **Turn on Restricted Mode**.

6. Create a password.

7. Confirm the password. **Restricted Mode** is now set.

TIP #156

Turn off Push Notifications

It can be a pain to get messages and noises from TikTok every time you get a new like, comment, follower, mention, direct message, new videos from accounts you follow, video suggestions from TikTok, and livestream notifications from accounts you follow. You can easily turn any or all of them off.

1. Go to your **Profile** screen.

2. Tap the **More** (. . .) icon in the top right hand corner.

3. Tap **Push notifications** under **General**. From here you can control when or if you get push notifications.

TIP #157

The Safety Center

From the **Privacy and settings** page, you can also find the **Safety Center**, which provides a lot of information on protecting yourself while using the app. You can also view TikTok's **Community Guidelines**, **Privacy Policy**, **Copyright Policy**, and **Terms of Use** from this screen.

TIP #158

Download Your Data

When you use TikTok, they collect information from you. You can request a copy of your data so you can see what they are collecting, although it could take up to a month to process your request. When you request your information, you can get:

- information about your profile, including your username, profile photo, profile description and contact information.
- information on your activity, including your videos, comments, chat history, purchase history, like list, favorite list, and more.
- information on your app settings.

1. Go to your **Profile** screen.

2. Tap the **More** (. . .) icon in the top right hand corner.

3. Tap **Privacy and safety**.

4. Tap **Personalization and data**.

5. Tap **Download your data**.

6. When the data is ready for viewing, you can find it on the **Download Data** tab at the top of the page.

TIP #159

Tell TikTok to Forget Your Login Information

By default, TikTok remembers and stores your username and password. That's all well and fine, but if you let others use your phone, you might wish to disable this feature.

1. From your **Profile** screen, tap the **More** (. . .) icon.

2. Tap **Manage my account**.

3. Deselect **Save login info**. Now, each time you shut down the app, you'll have to login.

YOU'RE IN CONTROL

Remember that from the **Privacy and safety** screen, you can also decide whether or not your videos can be downloaded, who can send you direct messages, who can **Duet** or **React** to your videos, and more. If you want more information, check out TikTok's educational video series, "You're in Control." These short videos are silly, but they do provide a visual understanding of how you can control your account and keep yourself as protected as you want and need to be.

ACCOUNT HACKED?

If your account password or phone number has been changed, your username or nickname has been changed, videos have been deleted or posted without your permission, or messages you didn't write are showing up, you have probably been hacked. Here's what you can do:

1. Change your password. This will lock out all other users who have hacked your account. If you can't change the password, contact the Support Team.

2. Check your account information: Go to the **More** (. . .) icon at the top right hand corner of the Profile screen. Tap on Settings and then Manage My Account to verify if the information is correct.

TAKING CARE OF HARASSMENT AND BULLYING

From trolls to unwanted or inappropriate comments, it's important that you feel safe within the TikTok community.

Here are some of the app settings that let you restrict unwanted community interactions:

- Make your account private (see page 119).
- Decide who can duet or react to your videos (page 109).
- Delete any comment by long pressing it.
- Delete a fan or block a user (page 120).
- Report the user.

TIP #160

How to Delete Your Account

Had enough? Do this.

1. Go to your **Profile** screen.

2. Tap the **More** (. . .) icon in the top right hand corner.

3. Tap **Manage my account**.

4. Tap **Delete account** at the bottom of the page. TikTok will send you a verification code to make sure it's actually you deleting the account.

TIP #161

Last, But Not Least

We hope the instructions and tips in this book help you to achieve what you want out of TikTok. Go viral, get famous, and make a ton of money, if that's what you're after. Throughout it all, make sure you're having fun. None of this is truly worth stressing out over. Know when to take a break, and even better, know when to walk away. And if you're taking care of yourself and still having fun, here's one last piece of advice: don't get left behind when the next big thing comes along. TikTok right now is IT. Tomorrow, it may be something else. If your grandmother has her own TikTok account, start searching for this next big thing and get in while it's still growing. Putting all your eggs in one basket will hurt your brand in the long run. Good luck and happy TikToking!

INDEX

reporting, 121
tagging, 93